Crisis and Change in World Politics

About the Book and Authors

This book analyses the impact of crises on international systems. It begins with an appraisal and formulation of key concepts, including system, crisis, stability, and equilibrium. The authors develop Indices of Severity and Importance for international crises that represent the crises' immediate and long-term effects on the process and structure of world politics. Each index encompasses a wide range of system components. The Severity Index takes into account actors, great power/ superpower involvement, geostrategic salience, heterogeneity among participants, issues, and extent of violence. The Importance Index incorporates changes in power, actors, rules, and alliances. A Crisis-as-Earthquake Model shows that severity can be used to predict importance, with each crisis measured on a 10-point Richter-type scale. Two penetrating case studies—the 1973–1974 Middle East Crisis and the 1975–1976 Angola Crisis—illustrate the application of the model in a specific context. These findings constitute a significant step forward in our ability to predict the consequences of international crises.

Michael Brecher is professor of political science at McGill University and director of the International Crisis Behavior Project. **Patrick James** is assistant professor of political science at McGill University.

Crisis and Change in World Politics

**Michael Brecher and
Patrick James**

Westview Press / Boulder and London

Copyright © 1986 by Westview Press, Inc.

Published in 1986 in the United States of America by Westview Press, Inc.; Frederick A. Praeger, Publisher; 5500 Central Avenue, Boulder, Colorado 80301

Library of Congress Cataloging-in-Publication Data
Brecher, Michael.
  Crisis and change in world politics.
  Bibliography: p.
  Includes index.
  1. International relations—Research. I. James,
Patrick, 1957– . II. Title.
JX1291.B725 1986   327′.072   86-4113
ISBN 0-8133-7211-9 (alk. paper)

Printed and bound in the United States of America

The paper used in this publication meets the requirements of the American National Standard for Permanence of Paper for Printed Library Materials Z39.48-1984.

10   9   8   7   6   5   4   3   2   1

Contents

Tables and Figures

Figures

Acknowledgments

This book was made possible by grants to the International Crisis Behaviour (ICB) Project from the Social Sciences and Humanities Research Council of Canada and by extended leaves of absence granted to Michael Brecher by McGill University. Different parts of the study have benefited greatly from comments by Yehudit Auerbach, Hemda Ben Yehuda, Jerome Black, Avraham Diskin, Steven Finestone, Robert Keohane, Sheila Moser, Jonathan Wilkenfeld, Yaacov Vertzberger, and Avner Yaniv. A preliminary and abbreviated version of Chapter appeared as M. Brecher and H. Ben Yehuda, "System and Crisis in International Politics," *Review of International Studies* 11, no. 1 (January 1985):17–36.

The following students performed valuable services as research assistants on this and other segments of the ICB Project: Hemda Ben Yehuda, Gerald Bichunsky, Mark Boyer, Diana Brecher, Daryll Clow, Doreen Duffy, Ofra Einav, Robert Einav, Alex Forma, Etel Goldmann, Sharon Greenblatt, Steve Hill, Tod Hoffman, Lawrence Katcher, Cindy Kite, Maureen Latimer, Eileen Long, Ester Long, Rutie Moser, Hanan Naveh, Arie Ofri, Lily Polliack, (the late) Mottie Raz, Michael Reichman, André Rosenthal, Joel Schleicher, Bruce Slawitsky, Laura Trinkl, and Sara Vertzberger.

Michael Brecher and Patrick James

Prologue

The need to explain change was cogently noted by W. E. Moore in the late 1960s: "Paradoxically, as the rate of social change has accelerated in the real world of experience, the scientific disciplines dealing with man's actions and products have tended to emphasize orderly interdependence and static continuity" (Moore, 1968:365). Clearly this statement applied to world politics, as well as to other domains of social science. Seemingly in response to this criticism, a marked shift in the focus of research has taken place from the static aspects of world politics to the dynamic concept of systemic change.[1]

Despite the increasing scholarly interest in change, there is no consensus on guiding themes. J. A. Vasquez and R. W. Mansbach (1983:257) recently asked: "Why does change occur, can it be controlled, where is it heading?" Earlier, P. J. Katzenstein (1975) analyzed the trends and changes in levels of interdependence among actors in world politics. R. O. Keohane and J. S. Nye (1977), along with O. R. Young (1982), explored the types of, and reasons for, regime transformation. And R. Gilpin (1981:2) examined the sources of intensive military conflict during periods of rapid economic and political upheavals, as well as the extent to which social, economic, and technological developments altered the role of war in the process of international political change.

This book is an effort to overcome the major obstacle to a creative system orientation in world politics—a dearth of knowledge about system-level change. In more specific terms, it will involve the study of international crisis and its role in change. To accomplish the principal objective, several tasks are essential.

The first is a set of exercises in the revision and formation of relevant concepts. The literature on international systems will be reviewed, culminating in a fundamental restatement of the meaning of international system. The focus will be on the dimensions relevant to systemic change. This section will be followed by an attempt to revitalize the classic concepts of stability and equilibrium, thereby providing the theoretical basis for the operationalization of crisis

1

severity and importance. We then turn to a macro-level definition of international crisis, derived from the redefinition of international system. A micro-level definition, focusing on the individual state actor, will be developed, and its linkage with international crisis as a whole will be specified.

These exercises in concept formation will facilitate the completion of a second task: the description of empirical indicators for the immediate severity and long-term importance of international crises. A third exercise will be the creation of indices of overall severity and importance, to be used in the analysis of crises as catalysts to systemic change, that is, as international earthquakes. In so doing, we attempt to develop for the field of world politics the counterpart of the measurement technique for the intensity (severity) of physical earthquakes—the Richter scale.

The fourth (and most ambitious) task is to predict the long-term importance of systemic crises on the basis of their immediate severity.[2] This task would take us beyond the assessment of immediate effects of earthquakes to their impact on the structure and process of the international system. Such an achievement would mark a major step forward in our ability to anticipate the likely consequences of future crises and to act in accord with the interests of world order.

1

Concepts

INTERNATIONAL SYSTEM

The concept of international system emerged from general systems theory, which began its assault on traditional modes of thinking in the social sciences during the 1950s. Since that time, a number of efforts have been directed toward concept formation. The following review of the literature on international systems, stability and equilibrium, and systemic crisis will reflect a certain purpose and a corresponding set of evaluative criteria. The objective is to derive a definition of systemic crisis that is valid, useful for the study of change, and analytically comprehensive. This definition must incorporate the crucial concepts related to change that permeate the literature. It should also focus attention on the sources of change at the international level, as opposed to merely describing structure and process. Finally, a viable definition of systemic crisis must connect the unit and system levels of analysis, to facilitate the comprehensive study of crisis-induced change.

Among the pioneers of systems theory, K. E. Boulding (1956:202, 201) introduced the idea of system rungs or levels by advocating "the arrangement of theoretical systems and constructs in a hierarchy of complexity, roughly corresponding to the complexity of the 'individuals' of the various empirical fields" and the development of "a level of abstraction appropriate to each." He then suggested nine levels of analysis, ranging from static structure, or "frameworks," through dynamic systems of "clockworks," all the way to social organizations, and, at the apex, "transcendental systems."

Among those who apply systems theory to the study of politics, K. W. Deutsch (1974:152–156) set out a 10-level political system. The first six levels are, in ascending order, individuals, nuclear families, extended kin groups, villages, towns, and cities. The four higher levels fall within the realm of international politics—small nation-states, middling nation-states, large nation-states, and the United Nations (UN). In terms of international systems the ninth level is crucial: It "brings us to the largest powers and to much of international politics."

In the study of world politics C. A. McClelland (1955:34; 1958) was perhaps the first to specify levels: nation-states; "larger systems called variously, the world society, the world market, the world community, etc."; and "the sub-systems of other nations." "International relations," he wrote, "should be investigated systematically at each level of relationship where transactions occur." Levels were implicitly recognized by K. N. Waltz (1959) through his three images of man, the state, and war. The "level-of-analysis problem," focusing on the international system and the nation-state, was given explicit formulation by J. D. Singer (1961). Elsewhere he noted half a dozen levels—the individual, primary, and secondary associations, national state, intergovernmental organizations of a regional, continental, or global nature, nongovernmental associations, and global system (1971:16–18). In the most general sense two levels may be designated: system, or macro, comprising the global system, the dominant system, and subsystems; and unit, or micro, comprising states and nonstate actors.

Definitions

No definition of international system is universally accepted by scholars. M. A. Kaplan (1957:4, 9), in a seminal work on world politics, referred to a "system of action" as

> a set of variables so related, in contradistinction to its environment, that describably behavioral regularities characterize the internal relationship of the variables to each other and the external relationships of the set of individual variables to combinations of external variables . . . the study of systems involves the study of relationships . . . [among] the following variables: the essential rules of the system, the transformation rules, the actor classificatory variables, the capability variables, and the information variables.

Less abstract and less complex is S. Hoffmann's formulation (1961:207):

> An international system is a pattern of relations between the basic units of world politics, which is characterized by the scope of the objectives pursued by those units and of the tasks performed among them, as well as by the means used in order to achieve these goals and perform those tasks. This pattern is largely determined by the structure of the world, the nature of forces which operate across or within the major units, and the capabilities, pattern of power, and political culture of those units.

An international system for Hoffmann is thus synonymous with the totality of international relations.

R. N. Rosecrance (1963:5, 6) also conceived of international relations in terms of separate systems. However, he focused on their distinguishing characteristics: "distinctive patterns, each enduring for a limited period of time and demarcated by significant changes in diplomatic style." R. Aron, whose approach in "Conflict and War from the Viewpoint of Historical Sociology" (1957) influenced the work of both Hoffmann and Rosecrance, emphasized (1966:95, 94) "the configuration of the relation of forces" among "a small number of actors" and declared: "I call an international system the ensemble constituted by political units that maintain regular relations with each other and that are all capable of being implicated in a generalized war. . . . The structure of international systems is always oligopolistic. In each period the principal actors have determined the system more than they have been determined by it."

A more explicit definition, which differentiates international systems from other phenomena in world politics, is that of E. B. Haas.

> Definitional clarity, verbal and operational, must obtain with respect to (1) the relationships being abstracted, i.e. the nature of the *inputs* and *outputs*; (2) the *units* of which the system is composed; (3) the *environment* surrounding the system; otherwise the boundaries of the system cannot be ascertained—and without boundaries we have no system; (4) the dominant *attributes* of the system, such as the question of whether the system is supposed to be in movement or in equilibrium, stable or revolutionary, self-maintaining or creatively adaptive; . . . (5) the *structures* that enable the system to perform; and finally (6) the *functions* the system is supposed to perform. (1964:62–63; emphasis in original)

The call for definitional clarity and the list of system properties were admirable steps, but alas, the links among them were not developed.

The important distinction between boundaries and environment is also evident in McClelland's definition (1966:20): "The conception of the international system is an expanded version of the notion of two-actors-in-interaction. . . . Any system is a structure that is perceived by its observers to have elements in interaction or relationships and some identifiable boundaries that separate it from its environment." However, just as Hoffmann erred by making the concept of system all inclusive, McClelland's definition was too restrictive; he confined system to interaction. Moreover, the terms system and structure appear to be synonymous.

O. R. Young (1968a:6) restored the balance by specifying four essential components of a system: "a group of actors standing in characteristic relationships to each other (structure), interacting on the basis of recognizable patterns (processes), and subject to various contextual limitations." His distinction between structure and process was blurred, however. Structure refers to "characteristic relationships" among the actors, but these relationships can also be understood to mean patterns of interaction. R. O. Keohane and J. S. Nye (1977:20–21) clarified this distinction as follows: "The *structure* of a system refers to the distribution of capabilities among similar units. In international political systems the most important units are states, and the relevant capabilities have been regarded as their power resources. . . . Structure is therefore distinguished from *process*, which refers to allocative or bargaining behavior within a power structure" (emphasis in original).

Waltz (1979:40) also asserted the need for a clearcut demarcation between structure and interaction. He used the former to refer to the distribution of power among the states in a system, whereas the latter indicates the dynamic processes among those actors. He includes structure and interaction in his definition of a system as "a set of interacting units. At one level, a system consists of a structure, and the structure is the systems-level component that makes it possible to think of the units as forming a set as distinct from a mere collection. At another level, the system consists of interacting units. The aim of systems theory is to show how the two levels operate and interact, and that requires marking them off from each other." In elaborating a theory of international politics, however, Waltz seemed to have replicated McClelland's error but at the other extreme of the spectrum—an overemphasis on structure.

The initial attempts to integrate system concepts into international relations theory resulted in exclusive or predominant attention to the great powers in world politics: Kaplan, Hoffmann, Rosecrance, Aron, Haas, McClelland, Young, Waltz, and others meant by the concept of international system either the global system or, more often, the dominant system, a synonym for J. D. Singer and M. Small's (1972:381) "Central Sub-System," that is, "the most powerful, industrialized, and diplomatically active members of the interstate system, generally coinciding with the 'European state system.' " This definition seemed to many scholars increasingly inadequate as the number of international actors doubled and then trebled with the end of empires in Asia and Africa.[3] Thus, in reaction, a new focus on subsystems emerged, with the rationale that "it is dangerous to assume that the elephants are the only members of the system or to ignore the squirrels by virtue of a specious claim that the elephants determine all or most of their actions" (Brecher, 1963:217). Furthermore, the subsystem was presented as a middle ground between the global or dominant system level and the nation-as-actor level of analysis in an attempt to combine the advantages of both and to minimize their disadvantages (Boals, 1973:399).

Subsystem: Geography

Two strands are present in the subsystems literature—geography and issue.[4] The case in favor of geography was made by Young (1968a:20): "Comparisons of . . . regional subsystems . . . might prove quite useful in studying such problems as the management of power, stability, and change in international politics." "The subordinate system, in the region," according to L. J. Cantori and S. J. Spiegel (1970:3 and fn. 3), "is the total interaction of relations within that region"; further, "we have used the term 'subordinate system' to apply to regions in order to stress the interactive nature of local areas."

Proponents of the first approach suggest various criteria to delineate subsystems, of which the most important is geographic proximity among actors. L. Binder (1958:415), the first to employ the concept of subordinate system, implied several components: (1) a geographic area; (2) greater influence of, or penetration from, the dominant system than the reverse; and (3) "extra-area power . . . 'refracted' when projected into the Middle Eastern element." G. Modelski (1961) was more precise in defining a regional subsystem as "a less than universal pattern of relationships created by a cluster of small powers in a condition of proximity." M. Brecher (1963:220), in quest of comprehensiveness, specified six conditions: (1) delimited scope, with primary emphasis on a geographic region; (2) at least three actors; (3) recognition by other actors that they constitute a distinctive community, region, or segment of the global system; (4) self-identification by the members as such; (5) inferiority of power to units in the dominant system; and (6) greater effect of changes in the dominant system on the subordinate system than the reverse. I. W. Zartman (1967:547) also noted a geographic region as an essential component and added an international organization and intrarelatedness or autonomy.

W. R. Thompson (1973) presented an inventory of 21 attributes of a geographic subsystem, derived from published articles on this concept between 1958 and 1971. Only 2 attributes—proximity and regular interaction—were cited consistently, in 18 of 22 papers. As for other criteria, such as intrarelatedness, recognition as a distinctive region, number of actors, configuration of power, shared bonds among the members, evidence of integration, common level of economic development, and so on, there was no consensus: Only 22 percent of the potential cells were checked in a dyadic index of interanalyst agreement. Even the labels vary. They include subordinate international system (Binder, 1958); subordinate state system (Brecher, 1963; Zartman, 1967; Bowman, 1968); regional subsystem (Modelski, 1961; Kaiser, 1968; Thompson, 1970; Yalem, 1970); international subsystem (Hellmann, 1969; E. Haas, 1970; Dominguez, 1971; Shepherd, 1970); subordinate system–international region (Cantori and Spiegel, 1970); and partial international system (Hoffmann, 1963). Results of empirical research on the Middle East subsystem reinforced this absence of uniformity: Twenty-six states were identified in five articles or books as belonging to the region—but no two lists were identical (Thompson, 1981:359). B. M. Russett, reaching the same conclusion (1967:182), cautioned against the careless use of geographic labels and added: "Our moral is that for purposes of generalization one should not refer to Asia unless one specifically means to refer to countries with a certain *physical* proximity to each other, and distance from the rest of the world" (emphasis in original). A geographic component with such a narrow meaning has limited theoretical utility.

Among the most careful in using a geographic criterion was M. Haas (1970:101), who derived a subsystem from an international system that he defined as "an aggregation of all politically autonomous and semi-autonomous societal systems; any subset of such entities, thus, constitutes an *international subsystem.*" In delineating its components, he revised Brecher's six elements as follows: (1) delimited scope, with primary emphasis on a geographic region; (2) at least two actors; and (3) a "relatively self-contained network of political interactions between the members, involving such activities as goal attainment, adaptation, pattern maintenance, and integration, and dealing with power relations and military interactions." His empirical analysis of 21 subsystems (1974:336–356) combined geographic and issue criteria, providing a rare link to the second strand in the subsystems literature.

Subsystem: Issue

The concept of issue system emerged gradually. One plausible explanation was suggested by P. D. Dean and J. A. Vasquez (1976:17): "The reason they do not examine different issues lies in the . . . assumption of the Realist paradigm . . . that all issues . . . can be treated as if there were only one unidimensional issue in the system— the struggle for power and peace." K. J. Holsti (1972:79, 80) challenged the realist view persuasively:

It is misleading today to view the structure of power and influence in the world as being polarized on all issues, for there are other problems in which quite different states are involved and where these two great powers [United States and USSR] have not assumed or appropriated leadership positions. . . . In brief, the structure of power and influence in the world . . . appears under different configurations depending upon the issue and geographic subsystems involved.

Building upon J. N. Rosenau's advocacy (1963:115 and fn. 4; 1966) of "central prominence to the concept of issue-areas" and his notion that there can be as many systems as there are issue-areas, W. F. Hanrieder (1965) argued that certain issues tend to give rise to bipolar relationships whereas other issues give rise to multipolar relationships—and that the concepts of bipolar and multipolar should therefore be used only to describe issue subsystems. Dean and Vasquez (1976:20) also suggested that the concept of system polarity "can be redefined as *the number of issues between actors*" (emphasis in original). Moreover, "the number of issues between actors is a function of actor perception."

The literature on issue subsystems is diverse. M. Haas (1974:328–329) explored the concept of international conflict subsystem, which "is composed of a set of actors with a relatively self-contained pattern of military articulation and aggregation of state interests, along with interstate planmaking, implementation, and any other functions characteristic of autonomous polities." Without explicitly mentioning issues, W. Zimmerman (1972:18) urged that regional subsystems may be differentiated and "by emphasizing behavioral criteria, i.e., by identifying norms especially pertaining to conflict management and resolution which are specific to a group of states." As examples he mentions the Warsaw Treaty Organization, the Council for Mutual Economic Assistance, and the Organization of American States (OAS). Interaction within various issue systems was addressed by Keohane and Nye (1977:25, 50–51):

The agenda of interstate relationships consists of multiple issues that are not arranged in a clear or consistent hierarchy. . . . Within each issue area one posits that states will pursue their relatively coherent self-interests and that stronger states in the issue system will dominate weaker ones and determine the rules of the game. Issue structuralism thus is capable of generating clear predictions for particular situations.

Russett (1967:11) presented an elaborate analysis of issue subsystems, conceptually and empirically, within the framework of international regions. These he designates in terms of five issue criteria: regions of social and cultural homogeneity; regions of states that share similar political attitudes or external behavior; regions of political interdependence with a network of political institutions; regions of economic interdependence; and regions of geographical proximity.

D. E. Lampert (1980:429–430) was the most direct in asserting the primacy of issue over geography as the basic component of subsystems:

> The approach employed herein stresses the importance of issues for understanding systems in global politics. . . . In certain contexts, this will mean going beyond the conventional wisdom of much regional analysis. Regional affinities, influence patterns, interdependencies, political cultures, and so forth are among the many sources of issues in world politics. Whether behavior involving them remains within the confines of a single region, transcends them, or engenders impacts felt around the world is really an empirical question.

In a recent critique of the literature on international systems D. A. Zinnes (1980) argued persuasively that a satisfactory definition must address two basic questions: (1) How do we know one when we see one? (2) What distinguishes one from another? The first requirement can be met by a revised definition that builds upon earlier writings but restores the balance between structure and process within an integrated set of system components. Generically,

> an international system is comprised of actors that are situated in a configuartion of power (*structure*), are involved in regular patterns of interaction (*process*), are separated from other units by *boundaries* set by a given *issue*, and are constrained in their behavior from within (*context*) and from outside the system (*environment*).

System Components

A system has both static and dynamic components. *Structure* refers to how the actors stand in relation to each other. Its basic variables are the number of actors and the distribution of power among them. *Process* designates the interaction patterns among the actors of a system. The basic interaction variables are type, identified along with conflict/cooperation dimension, and intensity, indicated by the volume of interaction during a given time period.[5] A link between structure and process is postulated: every structure has a corresponding interaction process; and a structure creates and maintains regular interaction.

International systems (and systemic crises) do not require the physical proximity of actors, though this trait is frequently present. Another distinctive property of an international system, which serves to demarcate its boundaries, is issue. This concept may be defined as a specific shared focus of interest for two or more actors. There are war-peace issues: K. J. Holsti (1972:452–455) noted several issues at the base of 77 international conflicts and crises from 1919 to 1965— territory; composition of a government; rights or privileges to bases; national honor; unlimited aggrandizement or imperialism; liberation; and unification. There are economic and developmental issues: Keohane and Nye (1977, Part 2) analyzed fishing, commercial navigation, offshore drilling, and military uses in the issue-area of oceans space and resources, as well as exchange rates, reserve assets, international capital movements, and adjustment, liquidity, and confidence in a regime, within the international monetary issue-area. There are also political, cultural, status, and technological issues, within broader categories of issue-areas (Potter, 1980).

The focus on subsystems enables us to resolve a paradox in the globally oriented traditional concept of international system and thereby to address the other system properties, namely, boundaries, context, and environment. The paradox is simple yet fundamental. By definition, every system has boundaries that demarcate members from other units. However, the global international system, which is coterminous with the planet earth, excludes a priori the possibility of nonmember units and, therefore, of boundaries. It has the additional shortcoming of negating the existence of an environment as a phe- nomenon distinct from the system itself. That in turn makes it impossible to distinguish between two kinds of effects on the behavior of actors—contextual, those arising from within the system, and environmental, those from outside. As Young (1968a:23) observed, a global system can be characterized only by its context since "there is nothing outside the system which can be labeled environment." The concept of environment, he continued, is useful when dealing with subsystems, for these "may be affected by various factors (including other organized entities) located outside its boundaries in spatial terms."

Typical of the all-inclusive view of world politics is the contention of M. A. East et al. (1978:145) that "international system variables must focus on patterns of interactions and relationships among all the major entities in the international system. In other words, the perspective is holistic and considers the system as a single unit." The first, partially successful critique of this approach took the form of the geographically based concept of subordinate system. As noted, its weaknesses were revealed by students of transnational relations and regimes. In modifying the realist paradigm of a universal struggle for power and peace and in their construct of issue systems, scholars of interdependence also postulate distinctive boundaries. In effect, though not in name, they focus on partial systems of subsystems.

The concept of boundaries is used in several ways in the world politics literature. They may be conceived in vertical terms, that is, boundaries in time, as with Rosecrance's (1963, Chap. 11) 9 international systems from 1740 to 1960 and M. Haas's (1974) 21 subsystems from 1649 to 1898. Boundaries may also be thought of as horizontal, that is, in spatial terms—the "conceptual or physical line marking the border between systems at the same level of analysis, as between a system and its environment" (Singer, 1971:12–13); this is reflected in the writings on regional systems previously discussed and on issue-areas, as in Rosenau (1966:74). A third focus is diagonal, that is, time and space boundaries together; in Rosenau's words (1972:149) the diagonal combines vertical and horizontal analysis "since it involves discerning trends across situations in terms of predispositions acquired down through history."

The notion of boundaries presented here is derived from the general concept of international system that has clearly designated issue boundaries, geographic or other. As such they make possible the spatial distinction between context and environment. The concepts of context and environment incorporate all geographic, political, military, technological, societal, and cultural elements that affect the structure and process of a system from within and from outside the system, respectively. These two concepts may be explored along two dimensions, extent of similarity and degree of integrativeness.

Without explicitly referring to context or differentiating similarity and integrativeness, Cantori and Spiegel (1970:10) discussed cohesion by which they meant "the degree of similarity or complementarity in the properties of the political entities being considered and the degree of interaction between these units." They thereby dealt with social, economic, political, and organizational cohesion within five regional systems, the Middle East, West Europe, Latin America, Southeast Asia, and West Africa. Brecher (1963:223–226, 230–232) also related these two dimensions. He discussed organizational integration as a structural feature of a subordinate system while addressing the extent of similarity under the rubric of textural features.

A review of the literature on international system—both macro-level and subsystem—has revealed great diversity and, on the surface, a lack of integration. An attempt to overcome this glaring deficiency has resulted in a fundamental reorientation in the concept of system and its necessary and sufficient components. The overarching redefinition of an international system and the six integral components (structure, process, boundaries, issue, context, and environment) provide a practical answer to the critical questions raised by Zinnes and countless others: How do we know one when we see one? What distinguishes one from another?

STABILITY AND EQUILIBRIUM

The revised definition of international system presented herein enables us to identify a system. The concepts needed to distinguish among systems are stability and equilibrium, system attributes that have been dealt with extensively in the international relations literature. In general, more emphasis has been given to stability; equilibrium has not been adequately defined nor has its relationship to stability been fully developed.

Kaplan (1957:6, 21, 35–36) initially acknowledged that "equilibrium and stability are not the same concepts." However, he established a link between them without first clearly indicating their meaning: "an equilibrium may be unstable. The stable equilibrium is the equilibrium that fluctuates within given limits." Moreover, he designated his six distinct international systems as "six states of equilibrium of an ultra-stable international system."[6] Thus equilibrium for Kaplan is synonymous with system. This identity is also evident in his consideration of the stability of a system. Stability is related to both structure and process:

> If an essential national actor develops supranational organizational objectives [change in interaction patterns], if a change in relative capabilities leads to positive feedback [change in structure], and so on, or if the attempt to implement one rule of the 'balance of power' system conflicts with the implementation of one or more of the remaining essential rules, the 'balance of power' system will become unstable.

This instability, in turn, will "shift it from its existing equilibrium . . . [and] transform it into a different system." Equilibrium is the normal state of a system; Kaplan's concern was with "the expectations for stability of each of the systems." Finally, disequilibrium has no place in Kaplan's model.

The first wave of analysts in the ongoing debate over the relationship between systemic polarity and systemic stability virtually omitted discussion of the concept of equilibrium (Waltz, 1964: Deutsch and Singer, 1964; Rosecrance, 1966; Young, 1968b). Typical were K. W. Deutsch and J. D. Singer (1964:390–392), who defined "stability as the probability that the system retains all of its essential characteristics; that no single nation becomes dominant; that most of its members continue to survive; and that large-scale war does not occur." They then made the jump to linguistic synonymity by referring to the "political definition of equilibrium that we have just proposed"— their sole reference to equilibrium. Finally, they termed their definition "quite compatible" with Kaplan's formulation of these concepts.

Among other theorists, Hoffmann (1961:208) distinguished between two types of system: "A stable system is one in which the stakes of conflict are limited . . . and the main actors agree on the rules according to which the competition will take place: a revolutionary system is one in which the incompatibility of purposes rules out such an agreement." He made no reference to equilibrium. Moreover, his definition was actor oriented, not systemic.

Aron (1966:100–101) barely mentioned stability and instability in distinguishing between homogeneous and heterogeneous systems. And although he discussed equilibrium extensively, he treated it as a policy, not a concept, which "is reduced to maneuvering in order to prevent a state from accumulating forces superior to those of its allied rivals. . . . This general rule is valid for all international systems."

For Rosecrance (1963:220–221) "a system aiming at stability" comprises four elements: "a source of disturbance or disruption (an input)"; a regulator; a list of environmental constraints; and outcomes. Of his nine international systems from 1740 to 1960, five were stable and four unstable. In a chapter entitled "Stability and Instability in the International System" he discussed "four major determinants of the international system" that "provide a clue to an understanding of stability and instability": direction, control, resources, and capacity. Although he emphasized interactions in his analysis of historical systems, Rosecrance was not explicit on the meaning of a regulator. He referred to "regularatory mechanisms [which] are found in formal or informal processes (the alliance system, balance of power mechanisms, a Concert of Europe, etc.)." However, these mechanisms may relate to structure or process or both. Finally, he made only a passing reference to equilibrium: "a secular tendency toward equilibrium does not emerge."

Young (1968a:42) was precise in defining stability both statically and dynamically:

In static terms, stability refers to the continuance of the essential variables of an international system (i.e. actors, structure, processes, and context) within the bounds of recognizability over time. Stability in this sense implies, therefore, an absence of qualitative changes. In dynamic terms, on the other hand, stability can be thought of as the tendency of a system to move in the direction of equilibrium following disturbances.

What is missing is the meaning of "qualitative changes" and the content of "equilibrium."

Waltz (1979:161–162) also was clear about the meaning of stability but defined this concept in static terms only: "To say that an international-political system is stable means two things: first, that it remains anarchic; second, that no consequential variations take place in the number of principal parties that constitute the system." This definition was consistent with that in an earlier paper in which Waltz related stability to structure as follows: "By 'structure' I mean the pattern according to which power is distributed; by 'stability,' the perpetuation of that structure without the occurrence of grossly destructive violence" (1967:229, fn. 18). Thus a change in structure means system transformation and new stability. Just as Kaplan equated system with equilibrium, so Waltz equated system with stability. Alas, he was silent on equilibrium.

Several international relations scholars, notably G. Liska, and D. G. Pruitt, did focus on equilibrium. In this they share the emphasis of general systems theorists and economists who identify stability and instability as states of equilibrium. Thus K. J. Arrow (1968:384, 387) referred to "the stability of competitive equilibrium" and "the stability of stationary equilibrium." Liska's definition (1957:11–12) was more general:

> Economic theory has generated or taken over from mechanics a whole typology of the equilibrum family in order to include in the concept developments that do not conform to the ideal of a self-maintaining system. It distinguishes between general and partial; unique and multiple; stable, neutral and unstable; long- and short-term; perfect and imperfect equilibrium; between equilibrium at a low and at a high level of employment, and the like.

Richardson's conception of stability "referred simply to any set of conditions under which the system would return to its equilibrium state; instability means to him any state of affairs that would not so return, but rather would continue to change until reaching some limit or breakdown point of the system" (Deutsch and Singer, 1964:391). Similarly, Liska (1957:13), in presenting "the barest outline of an equilibrium theory of international organization of security and international relations in general," declared: "I shall rely mainly on the ideas of progressive, stable, and unstable equilibrium."

Pruitt (1969:20, 23–24, 36–37) rigorously addressed the relationship of these concepts: "Instability is defined as the *likelihood of sudden (basic) change* and stability is defined as the opposite of instability" (emphasis in original). In analyzing Richardson's reaction systems in an arms race model, he noted: "At the point where the two lines intersect, the leaders of both nations will be satisfied. This point . . . is comparable to an equilibrium in physics in that it can be stable or unstable." Finally, "stable relations are usually characterized by oscillations around an equilibrium point. . . . Instability can be defined as the likelihood of sudden change and hence as the likelihood that one party will go 'too far.' " Pruitt was, in short, very clear on relationships but less so on the meaning of change and equilibrium.

In the mainstream literature on international systems the concept of equilibrium has been relegated to virtual obscurity.[7] The argument proposed here is that equilibrium must necessarily be restored to a coequal status with stability among the attributes of an international system, as a precondition to revising the concept of systemic crisis. Closely related tasks are formulating precise definitions that differentiate between stability and equilibrium and specifying the relationships between them; these definitions will permit us to distinguish among international systems.

The concept of change is the key to the distinction between stability and equilibrium, as well as to the organic link between them. *Change* may be defined as a shift from, or an alteration of, an existing pattern of interaction between two or more actors in the direction of greater conflict or cooperation. It is indicated by acts or events that exceed the bounds of normal fluctuations or a "normal relations range" (Azar, 1972; Azar et al., 1977:196–197, 207). Following W. R. Ashby (1952:87), four types of change may be distinguished: full function, which has no finite intervals of constancy; part function, which has finite intervals of change and finite intervals of constancy; step function, which has finite intervals of constancy separated by instantaneous jumps; null function, which shows no change over the whole period of observation. Change may also occur in the structure of a system, namely, as an increase or decrease in the number of actors and/or a shift in the distribution of power among them.

Stability may be defined as change within explicit bounds. *Instability* designates change beyond a normal fluctuation range. These concepts may be operationalized in terms of the quantity (number) of change(s) in the structure of a system, its process, or both, ranging from no changes to many changes. This continuum denotes degrees of stability. The absence of change indicates pure stability; its presence, some degree of instability. Any system can thus be designated as stable or unstable. Instability in the international system can be illustrated by change in the volume of interaction inherent in such phenomena as wars or crises involving essential actors. The presence of one of these processes may also induce structural change and thereby accentuate system instability.

Equilibrium may be defined as the steady state of a system, denoting change below the threshold of reversibility. *Disequilibrium* designates change beyond the threshold of reversibility. This meaning is broader than the notion of balance of power, a widely used synonym for equilibrium in the world politics literature. These concepts may be operationalized in terms of the quality (significance) of change in structure, process, or both, ranging from total reversibility to total irreversibility. This continuum denotes degrees of equilibrium. Incremental change indicates a state of equilibrium that has no effect on the system as a whole. Steplevel (irreversible) change indicates disequilibrium, which inevitably leads to system transformation, that is, a change in essential actors and/or the distribution of power among them. The new system, with properties that significantly differ from those of its predecessor, denotes a new equilibrium, that is, changes within it which are reversible. These system attributes are presented in Figure 1.

Every system has explicit or implicit rules of the game. Many international systems permit resort to violence as an instrument of crisis management; its legitimacy is derived from the legal sovereignty of international actors. This is evident in the inherent right of individual and collective self-defense, enshrined in the international institutions of the twentieth-century balance of power system (League of Nations) and bipolar system (United Nations). Violence that exceeds the bounds of a normal fluctuation range, even when legitimized by the rules of the game, constitutes, in our terms, instability but not disequilibrium, unless this violence challenges the structure of the system.

Acute distortions in an existing structure, process, or both may, or may not, lead to disequilibrium. Thus disequilibrium, ipso facto, denotes a high level of instability, but the reverse does not necessarily apply. This potential linkage was illuminated by Keohane (1981).

A "distortion" [i.e., instability] *per se*—an increase in temperature in an air-conditioned room, the rise of a single powerful state in a balance of power system, or a sharp increase in price because of a sudden upsurge in demand—does not suggest that a system is in disequilibrium: rather, it tests that hypothesis by allowing us to see whether adjustments take place. Does the air-conditioning bring the temperature back to the normal level, do coalitions form to counter the power of the rising

FIGURE 1 <u>Stability and Equilibrium</u>

A. <u>Stability : Quantity (Number) of Changes</u>

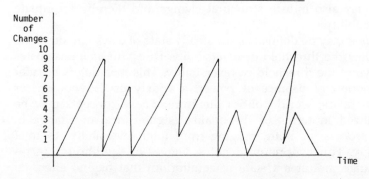

B. <u>Equilibrium : Quality (Type) of Changes</u>

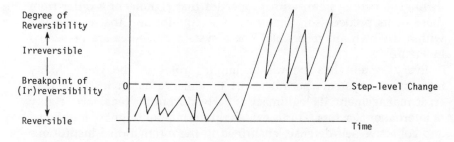

state, do new sources of supply appear in response to price increases?
. . . Disequilibrium of a system . . . appears only when the "forces
tending to restore the balance" (Arrow's phrase in a discussion of
equilibrium) fail to operate. Air-conditioning that heats a room to 100
degrees F.; "bandwagoning" that leads to hegemony by a single power;
prices that rise sharply and continuously without bringing forth new
supply—these are indications of disequilibrium.

There are additional linkages. Four states of a system, along with
illustrations and systemic outcomes, are presented in Table 1.

In summary, approaches to international systems have been assessed. A revised definition has been proposed based upon six system
components—actors, structure, process, boundaries, context, and environment. Furthermore, the two basic system attributes—stability
and equilibrium—have been redefined and the links between them
specified. Thus the dual task of identifying and differentiating systems
has now been completed.

TABLE 1

System Attributes: Links

		EQUILIBRIUM	DISEQUILIBRIUM
STABILITY	A	No change or few reversible changes in either structure or process and thus no effect on the system as a whole	Few irreversible changes in either structure or process which lead to system transformation
	B	Ideologically-based coalition groups in bipolar system and flexible alignment patterns in balance of power system preserve existing structure	Exit of major actor from bloc leading to loosening of bloc system and basic change in system polarity
	C	System unchanged	System transformed: new Equilibrium
INSTABILITY	A	Many but reversible changes in structure or process or both which do not lead to system transformation	Many irreversible changes in structure, process or both which lead to system transformation
	B	Limited wars in a multipolar or bipolar system	World war – likely to lead to destruction of existing structure, in either multipolar or bipolar system
	C	System unchanged: Equilibrium maintained, Stability restored	System transformed: new Equilibrium, new Stability

Code: A = State of the System
      B = Illustration
      C = System Outcome

INTERNATIONAL CRISIS

Existing definitions of international crisis are based upon concepts derived from the international systems and subsystems literature. They can be classified into two types: (1) process; (2) combined interaction-structure.

Process definitions view international crisis as a turning point at which an unusually intense period of conflictual interactions occurs. According to McClelland (1968:160–161), "a crisis is, in some way, a 'change of state' in the flow of international political actions. . . . Acute international crises are 'short burst' affairs and are marked by an unusual volume and intensity of events." Elsewhere (1972:6, 7) he referred to crisis as "an unusual manifestation of the interflow of activity between the participants." Moreover, crisis "interaction is likely to [take the form of effects on the] stability or equilibrium of the system, or disturbance of the normal run of business conducted between actors." Similarly, E. E. Azar (1972:184) defined a crisis in terms of interaction above the threshold of a "normal relations range" (NRR): "Interaction above the present upper critical threshold . . . for more than a very short time implies that a crisis situation has set in." These definitions tend to emphasize various stages of conflictual behavior among states; to characterize different types of activity; to measure the direction and speed of behavioral change; and to locate shifts that indicate changes in interaction processes.

Research associated with these definitions is highly descriptive. Well-operationalized concepts exist (Azar, 1975; Azar, Brody, and McClelland, 1972). And scales facilitate the ranking of various behavioral groups (Azar et al., 1977; Carson, 1970; McClelland, 1969; Tanter, 1966). The principal shortcomings are analytical. The logic for designating the beginning and end of a crisis was not precisely indicated. Changes in process were not related to structure. There was no attempt to uncover causes and effects of systemic crisis. The result is a group of studies more valuable for their empirical findings than for the understanding of the phenomenon of systemic crisis (e.g., Azar, 1972; Burgess and Lawton, 1972; Eckhardt and Azar, 1978; McClelland, 1968, 1972; Peterson, 1975; Tanter, 1974; Wilkenfeld, 1972).

Combined structural-interaction definitions view an international crisis as a situation characterized by basic change in processes that might affect structural variables of a system. According to C. F. Hermann (1972:10), "In any given international political system, critical variables must be maintained within certain limits or the instability of the system will be greatly increased—perhaps to the point where a new system will be formed. A crisis is a situation which disrupts the system or some part of the system." Young (1968c:15) expressed a similar view: "A crisis in international politics is a process of interaction occurring at higher levels of perceived intensity than the ordinary flow of events and characterized by . . . significant implications for the stability of some system or subsystem." Integrating structure into a process definition serves as a good analytical starting point by specifying the essential conditions and effects of crisis situations. There is, however, a serious limitation—little operationalization of the crucial concept of structure. The result is highly abstract, theoretical writings, which have not been followed by empirical research. The promise of superior conceptualization remains unfulfilled because, on the basis of the above-noted definition, it is difficult to say what structural change would amount to in operational terms. Nevertheless, by utilizing the dynamic component of interaction with a focus on the effects on structure, Hermann's and Young's definitions of systemic crisis are the best existing ones. In at least a relative sense, the Hermann and Young definitions are valid and analytically compre-hensive.

For another group, including Kaplan, Pruitt, and Waltz, systems are characterized by normal periods of equilibrium and stability with occasional shifts to disequilibrium and instability. Although such situations are not explicitly termed systemic crises, these transitions are clearly related to the concept of crisis. Except for Kaplan, however, the exponents of this view tended to deal with static rather than dynamic aspects of systems; that is, they emphasized the traits of a specific system, not the changes from one system to another.

A problem common to international crisis definitions is the mixture of unit- and system-level concepts. Young (1968c:10, 14) was a conspicuous offender, defining systemic crises as "situations perceived by the participants as much more competitive than the ordinary flow of international politics." Moreover, he stated that "crisis concerns the probabilities that violence of major proportions will break out," a point that "explicitly refers to subjective perceptions about the prospects of violence rather than to a more objective measure of the probability of violence." Another striking illustration is A. M. Wiener and H. Kahn's (1962) listing of twelve generic dimensions of crisis. This delineation includes system-level indicators such as a turning point in a sequence of events, a new configuration of international politics as a crisis outcome, and changes in relations among actors. There are also unit-level indicators: a perceived threat to actor goals; a sense of urgency, stress, and anxiety among decisionmakers; increased time pressure; and so on. A system-level definition of crisis should not include unit-level components such as perception, stress, and values.

In summary, several shortcomings are present in existing system-level definitions of crisis.

1. They are not effectively linked to the main body of the systems and subsystems literature; that is, they do not integrate all the key concepts—change in interaction, type of structure, degree of disequilibrium, and instability.

2. System-level definitions of crisis better serve descriptive than analytical purposes. These definitions focus clearly on interaction processes but do little to explain their sources and diverse effects on the properties of a system.

3. Despite a frequent mix of unit and system concepts there has been little attempt to link definitions at the two levels of crisis (McCormick, 1978; Tanter, 1978). The two main approaches to crisis research have not converged, and their findings have been, at best, partial.

In an effort to overcome these weaknesses we present a new definition of international crisis based upon the system properties discussed in the preceding sections. An international crisis may be defined as a situational change in an international system characterized by two individually necessary and collectively sufficient conditions: (1) distortion in the type and an increase in the intensity of disruptive interactions, with a high probability of military hostilities; and (2) a challenge to the existing structure of the system. This definition refers to international crises in the military-security (war-peace) issue-area only. Conditions (1) and (2) denote a higher-than-average increase in intensity of interactions and strain to the structure. By average we mean normal fluctuations (as discussed) that is, those that do not go beyond the bounds of the steady state of the system. Systemic crisis encompasses change. It is recognized that system change need not occur by leaps and jumps; it may result from aggregate or cumulative events. However, such change is the product of something other than a crisis.

The definition presented here specifies change in the system components, process, and structure. As such it enables us to differentiate three phases of an international crisis—pre-crisis, crisis, and post-crisis. Our definition is also linked to the system attributes, stability and equilibrium, for these conditions indicate a shift in the state of the system from stability-equilibrium to instability-equilibrium or stability-disequilibrium or instability-disequilibrium (illustrated in Table 1). In schematic terms, few distortions in process or few challenges to the structure denote low instability, whereas many changes indicate high instability; minor distortions (reversible) in process or minor challenges to the structure denote equilibrium, whereas major changes (irreversible) indicate disequilibrium. Instability, defined as change beyond a normal fluctuation range but within bounds, is present in all international crises; disequilibrium (irreversible change) is not.

The two crisis conditions and the linkages among system properties can be illustrated by the Berlin Blockade Crisis of 1948–1949. Tension between the Western Powers and the Soviet Union centered on the issue of occupied Germany. The 1945 Potsdam Agreement had divided Germany into four zones but had not provided that they were to be treated as one economic unit under the Allied Control Council. On 7 June 1948 the three Western Powers published the recommendations of the March 1948 London Conference (to which the Soviet Union had not been invited), calling for a merger of their zones in Germany. This conflictual act broke an existing though fragile East-West consensus on Germany and set in motion several changes in rapid succession. The Soviet Union responded on 24 June by blocking all Western transportation into and out of Berlin. President Harry S Truman countered on 26 June with an order to step up the airlift into Berlin, which had begun two months earlier, and continued with plans for the rehabilitation of Germany as part of Western Europe. These events mark a change in interaction pattern from low instability to high instability. Talks between the crisis actors began on 2 August 1948. An informal consensus on the future of Germany was reached on 21 March 1949 by the Four Powers—the United States, USSR, Great Britain, and France. An agreement was signed on 12 May formalizing the partition of Germany. These events indicated an accommodation by the system; the last event marked the end of the Berlin Crisis.

The 1948 Berlin Crisis also illustrates the links between crisis conditions and the system attributes of equilibrium and stability. The conditions postulate an increase in the quantity of distortions. Therefore any systemic crisis generates some degree of instability. In the Berlin case an increase in conflictual interactions occurred between the Western Powers and the USSR; that is, instability is evident between 7 June 1948 and 12 May 1949.

In international crises changes vary in quality as well as in quantity: In some cases they are reversible; in others they are irreversible. Thus a certain degree of disequilibrium is evident in the latter leading to system transformation. Distortions during the Berlin Crisis were step-level in nature; neither the interaction pattern nor the structure of the dominant system in world politics at the time was the same before and after the crisis. The agreement of 12 May 1949 illustrates this point. It left Germany divided, creating the foundation of two new international actors, the Federal Republic of Germany (FRG) and the German Democratic Republic (GDR), and changed the balance of power between the superpowers. Furthermore, the interaction pattern between the Western Powers and the Soviet Union after the agreement on Berlin came into effect differed substantially from that during the occupation of Germany by the Four Powers.

The dominant system during the Berlin Crisis was in a state of instability-disequilibrium. As such it helped to catalyze the transformation of the global system of embryonic bipolarity (1945–1948) to that of tight bipolarity. In that sense, the formation of the North Atlantic Treaty Organization (NATO) near the end of the crisis cannot be dismissed as a coincidence. This organization signaled the crystallization of a U.S.-led alliance that had the preservation of an independent Western Europe (including the emerging Federal Republic of Germany and its enclave in Berlin) as its fundamental objective.

Of course, it could be an exaggeration to claim that the Berlin Blockade Crisis alone triggered an event so momentous as the creation of NATO or caused the permanent division of Germany. But from a vantage point nearly four decades after that crisis, the changes catalyzed by it appear to be irreversible. This is true especially of the creation of two Germanies and the institutionalization of a U.S.-led and European-centered coalition.

The threshold events between phases of the crisis, as well as the overall links between crisis conditions and the system attributes of equilibrium and stability, are summarized in Table 2.

Having illustrated the properties of the definition of an international crisis through the 1948-1949 Berlin case, some modifying remarks are in order. A critic might ask why this definition has been derived and explained at such length when other explicit definitions (and frameworks) already exist. The reason is that none of the available options is entirely suitable for the range of purposes at issue. Some definitions emphasize process over structure (those of McClelland and Azar). Others include structure but not in a manner that would facilitate its operationalization (those of Hermann and Young). In still further cases, the concepts pertain to static rather than dynamic aspects of the international system (those of Pruitt and Waltz). Accordingly, the definition of international crisis presented here should be regarded as an attempt to synthesize the ongoing concerns of systemic analysis in a way especially useful for the study of change in world politics.

One other qualification should be made with respect to the new definition of international crisis. Some might object to the emphasis on military-security issues, pointing out that economic processes can

TABLE 2

Systemic Crisis and System Properties: Berlin 1948-49

Crisis Phase	System Components		System Attributes	
	Interaction	Structure	Stability	Equilibrium
Pre-Crisis	interaction among the powers ruling Germany within a normal relations range	embryonic bipolarity	Stable	Equilibrium
Crisis (7 June 1948-21 March 1949)	rapid increase in (irreversible) conflictual interaction between the USSR and the Western Powers	grave challenge to the existing structure	Unstable	Disequilibrium
Post-Crisis (21 March- 12 May 1949)	decline in conflictual interaction and an accommodation among the crisis actors	tight bipolarity	Stable	(New) Equilibrium

produce significant changes at the international level. Although the present definition focuses on dilemmas of war and peace, at least some international crises reflect the prior and cumulative impact of conflicting economic interests. Cod War I in 1973, a crisis that involved Iceland and the United Kingdom, is a useful example. This crisis, which included the use of violence, had a prior basis in a conflict over fishing rights—clearly an economic issue. Further instances of military-security crises resulting from clashing economic interests are noted elsewhere (Brecher, Wilkenfeld, and Moser, forthcoming). Hence the proposed definition does not exclude economic issues, although these factors can bring about change in other ways than through a military-security systemic crisis. Finally, it is hoped that this exercise will encourage new approaches to the study of international economic crises.

UNIT-SYSTEM LINKAGES

In all branches of knowledge there are several levels of analysis, each with distinct concepts, research questions, and methodologies. Analysis at every level is capable of illuminating a segment of knowledge within a discipline but no more. To provide insights into a part of any whole is admirable. However, the ultimate challenge is to link the findings at all levels into an aggregate of the whole and its parts in order to comprehend as much as possible of the total universe of knowledge in any field.

This perspective derives from a conviction that the competitive focus on a single level of analysis is counterproductive, just as the debate between qualitative and quantitative methods errs in failing to recognize the legitimate role of both. To examine the two levels—unit and system—would enable us to move beyond the position of blind men attempting to grasp the elephant. In this spirit we now confront the major task of linking the unit (micro) and system (macro) levels of crisis analysis, conceptually and empirically.

Since the early 1960s a large body of research has accumulated on state behavior in international crisis, the counterpart to studies of conflictual interactions among adversary states (Holsti, Siverson, and George, 1980; Tanter, 1975, 1978). The authors of these studies differ in their definitions, conceptual frameworks, and techniques of analysis. This book emphasizes points of convergence while maintaining a clearcut distinction between the two levels and their diverse effects. The distinction is expressed in the conceptual definitions, the operational specifications, and the focus of research.

A unit-level crisis derives from perceptions whereas an international crisis is objective. Stated differently, the focus of the former is image and action whereas that of the latter is reality and interaction. There is no one-to-one relationship between unit and international crises: The former occurs for a single state; the latter is predicated upon the existence of distortion in the pattern of interaction between two or more adversaries in a system.

A definition of international crisis has already been presented. From the perspective of a single state a crisis is a situation with three necessary and sufficient conditions, deriving from a change in its external or internal environment. All three are perceptions held by the highest-level decisionmakers:

1. A threat to basic values.
2. A simultaneous or subsequent high probability of involvement in military hostilities.
3. The awareness of finite time for response to the external value threat.[8]

At the unit level there are crisis actors, that is, states whose decisionmakers perceive the three conditions of crisis. These perceived conditions are considered to be interrelated and mutually reinforcing. This is especially worth noting with respect to the first and second conditions because it could be argued that a high probability of military hostilities will constitute a threat to basic values in and of itself. However, as Brecher (1978:17 and fn. 6) noted, "It may be postulated that the more active and/or the stronger the threat and/ or the more central (basic) the value(s) threatened, the higher will be the perceived probability that military hostilities will ensue. That, in turn, would lead to more intense perception of crisis." Furthermore, military hostilities "may be brief, marginal in resource allocation and peripheral in terms of the state's total responsive behavior during a crisis." Thus it would be inappropriate to exclude the content of the value threat from the defining conditions simply because a high probability of military hostilities poses a threat of some kind.

The unit-level conditions parallel those at the system level.[9] For the component of threat the counterparts are values of decisionmakers and structure of the system. Basic values, such as existence, influence in the global and/or regional systems, territorial integrity, economic welfare, and others, are the unit-level foundations on which foreign policy goals and behavior rest. They are the elements that guide decisions and actions of states. Similarly, at the system level, structure provides the setting for continuity in interaction processes. Threat at the unit level indicates (subjective) perceptions by decisionmakers. Challenge at the system level means an (objective) possibility of change in the structure. A challenge to the structure may or may not materialize just as a threat to basic values may or may not be realized.

In the Berlin Crisis the threat to Soviet and U.S. influence in the international system was followed by an increase in conflictual interaction. This distortion posed a challenge to the existing structure of the system, namely, to the number of actors (the question of a united Germany) and the distribution of power between the superpowers as a result of the crisis.

A rise in disruptive interaction is the system counterpart of an increase in perceived likelihood of military hostilities. By pursuing the example of the Berlin Crisis, events data on conflictual activity presented in the form of an event chronology (Corson, 1970; Tanter, 1974) can be used to locate changes in interaction processes and can be linked to the way these hostile acts affect basic values as perceived by decisionmakers.

A crisis may thus be addressed by an approach defined in either macro and micro terms. The former deals with a system as a whole; the latter focuses on each crisis actor. There are situational changes in which only one state perceives a crisis for itself, that is, actions by one (or more) state(s) that trigger images of threat, time, and war likelihood for a single actor, for example, the massing of Indian demonstrators on the border with Goa in 1955, creating a crisis for

TABLE 3

Static and Dynamic Concepts of Crisis

Nature of Concept \ Crisis Level	Unit	System
Static	trigger/termination	breakpoint/exitpoint
Dynamic	escalation/de-escalation	distortion/accommodation

Portugal. In other instances, two or more states experience a crisis over the same issue, as did the Western Powers and the USSR over Berlin in 1948-1949, 1959, and 1961.

The link between unit- and system-level concepts of crisis may be illustrated by two different cases: when a crisis for all actors is identical in time and when their crises overlap but are not identical in time. Establishing this link requires the clarification of dynamic and static concepts at both levels. The former deal with escalation/deescalation at the unit level and distortion/accommodation at the system level. The latter deal with trigger/termination and breakpoint/exitpoint, respectively. These concepts are presented in Table 3.

At the unit level, a trigger, a static act, is defined as the catalyst to a crisis. In the Berlin Crisis the trigger to the Soviet Union's crisis was the publication by the Western Powers on 7 June 1948 of the recommendations of the March London Conference. The trigger for the United States, Britain, and France was the Soviet decision on 24 June to block all Western transportation into and out of Berlin. In terms of a dynamic process, a trigger denotes an escalation in perceived threat, time pressure, and war likelihood.

The termination of a crisis, at the unit level, is defined as the point in time when decisionmakers' perceptions of threat, time pressure, and war likelihood decline to the level existing prior to the crisis trigger.[10] In the Berlin case the termination date for each of the Four Powers was 12 May 1949, when an agreement regarding West and East Germany as separate entities was signed. Thus although the triggers did not coincide, the termination dates for the various actors did. In dynamic process terms, termination for crisis actors marks the final deescalation in perceived threat, time pressure, and war likelihood during a crisis.

At the system level, parallel notions exist—breakpoint and exitpoint as counterparts of trigger and termination. A breakpoint is a disturbance to the system created by the entry of an actor into a crisis. A systemic crisis erupts with an initial breakpoint event, such as the Western Powers' challenge to Moscow on 7 June 1948 regarding the integration of their zones of occupation. In dynamic terms, this change denoted distortion in the pattern of East-West interaction. Similarly, an exitpoint refers to a significant reduction in conflictual activity, such as the formal agreement among the Four Powers on 12 May 1949 about the future of Germany and the lifting of the blockade. This change indicates accommodation, that is, a shift to a less intense level of interaction than that during the crisis.

When it has been established that an international crisis has occurred, its duration is measured from the first breakpoint to the last exitpoint, which, in unit-level terms, means from the trigger for the first actor to the termination for the last actor. These systemic concepts require greater elaboration.

For the initial breakpoint to occur there must be two or more adversarial actors in higher than normal conflictual interaction at the outset of a systemic crisis. They may both be crisis actors, a rare occurrence for this requires triggers on the same day, as in the 1965 India-Pakistan Crisis over Kutch.[11] They may include one crisis actor and one adversary that triggers the crisis and that later becomes a crisis actor itself, as with the Congo and Belgium in the 1960 Congo Crisis.[12] A variant is one crisis actor and one adversary with the latter joined by another in the process of becoming crisis actors, as with the United States and the USSR cum Cuba in the 1962 Missile Crisis.[13] Another possibility is one crisis actor at the outset with several adversaries who later become crisis actors simultaneously, as with the USSR and the United States-Britain-France in the 1948-1949 Berlin Crisis. As for the winding down of a systemic crisis, the overwhelming majority of cases reveal a simultaneous termination for all crisis actors and, therefore, simultaneous accommodation by the system, as in the Berlin, Cuba, and India-Pakistan cases.

Distortion and accommodation may be gradual or rapid. In general, international crises are characterized by multiple breakpoints (gradual distortion) and few exitpoints (rapid accommodation). The reason for this contrast is that the onset of a systemic crisis is usually a process in which crisis actors cumulatively challenge one another. The result is that breakpoints tend to differ in time, and distortion is therefore gradual. Accommodation, however, usually requires agreement, either formal or tacit. Thus exitpoints tend to coincide in time. However, as long as any crisis actor has not terminated its unit-level crisis, the systemic crisis may be said to continue: Accommodation has not yet been completed. In all cases the termination of the unit-level crisis for the last participant and the end of the international crisis are identical in time.

Breakpoints and exitpoints also indicate the addition or reduction of actors, respectively, in an international crisis. Each breakpoint denotes an increase in conflictual interaction relative to the pre-crisis phase whereas exitpoints signal accommodation at the system level. Linking unit upward to system, the effects of trigger/termination on breakpoints/exitpoints are immediate and direct; that is, a trigger at the unit level always denotes a breakpoint at the system level and thus a further distortion in international interaction.[14] In the Berlin case, the events on both 7 June and 24 June 1948, which were triggers at the unit level for the Soviet Union and the Western Powers, respectively, were also immediate breakpoints in the system-level crisis. However, when international crisis is linked downward to unit-level actors, the effects of exitpoints on deescalation are immediate and direct for some but may be indirect and protracted for others. Stated differently, not all system-level changes affect all units at once and equally in a readily identifiable way. The Berlin Crisis provides an example of direct and immediate effects of systemic change on unit-level crisis: The last systemic exitpoint on 12 May 1949 denotes final de-escalation for the Four Powers. In general, international crises have more significant effects than unit-level crises because they pose a dual danger—to the structure of the system and to its actors—whereas unit-level crises affect actors only.

In summary, an international crisis requires behavioral change on the part of at least two adversarial actors leading to more intense conflictual interaction. Although a crisis is catalyzed by behavioral actions, these actions, the trigger to a unit-level crisis, can always be traced to their perceptual origin. Here lies the organic link between the two levels of crisis.

2

Indicators

SEVERITY AND IMPORTANCE: AN OVERVIEW

What differentiates one international crisis from others, for example, crises over Suez (1956-1957), the Prague Spring (1968), the El Salvador–Honduras Football War (1969), Bangladesh (1971), the Falkland Islands (1982), or any international crisis since the onset of the Depression era? As a basic structural characteristic, the number of crisis actors is certainly relevant, that is, the number of states whose principal decisionmakers perceive a situational change as a threat to one or more of their basic values, as requiring a response within a finite time and as likely to involve them in military hostilities before the challenge has been overcome. Crises also differ in the extent of heterogeneity among the adversaries. Do they vary in military capability or are they all major (or minor) powers? Are they states with advanced or premodern economies or do they exhibit various levels of development? Are their political regimes divergent or similar? And do they reflect one or more cultures and belief systems?

There are other ways to distinguish among international crises. What is the extent of involvement by the superpowers: Is it primarily political or economic or military support for one or more of the adversaries, or did the United States/USSR engage in direct military intervention? Is the crisis's location of high or low geostrategic salience to one or more members of the international system? What are the issues at stake; are they military, political, economic, or cultural, or several of these combined? Is there interstate violence in the crisis; if so, how extensive is it?

These questions relate to the intensity of an international crisis from its outbreak to its conclusion. The variables concerned—ranging from the number of actors to the role of violence—effectively provide a unit-system linkage in the assessment of severity. The number of crisis actors (i.e., those whose decisionmakers perceive threat, time pressure, and war likelihood) has an obvious connection to the unit level. Another unit-level factor is superpower involvement, based upon the characteristics of relevant nation-states. At the systemic level, geostrategic salience and the range of issues combine to represent the structural component, whereas the extent of interstate violence corresponds to process or patterns of interaction. One indicator, heterogeneity, is a synthesis of the two levels, with, for example, culture at the unit level and relative military capability at the systemic level. Thus, the six indicators collectively encompass a wide range of unit and system-level sources of crisis intensity. Crises also differ in their long-term effects upon international systems. More specifically, some crises lead to the creation of one or more new states or the elimination of existing ones, or to a fundamental change in regime type or orientation within one or more actors; others do not. Some crises affect the configuration of alliances within an international system by creating a new alliance or destroying an existing one or by affecting the composition and/or cohesion of alliances that remain; others have no effect on alliances. Some crises lead to changes in the distribution of power among states; others do not. And some crises bring about a change in the existing rules of the game for state behavior; others do not. These four areas of system change provide the bases for measuring the consequences of international or systemic crises.

In summary, the attributes that indicate the overall severity or intensity of a crisis as a catalyst to system change are the number of crisis actors; the extent of heterogeneity among them; the range of issues in dispute; its scope of geostrategic salience; the type of superpower/major power involvement; and the level of violence among the crisis adversaries. The extent of durable change, that is, the overall importance or consequences of a crisis, is measured by four structural indicators of system change: change in the number of actors or their regime type or orientation; change in aspects of alliance configuration; change in the distribution of power among states; and change in the systemic rules of the game obtaining at the time.

The two dimensions of crisis, namely, severity and importance, refer to different types of change in different time frames. Severity is a composite of crisis attributes from the onset to the termination of a systemic crisis. The term refers to the volume of change among crisis participants and thus denotes the extent of system instability during a crisis. Importance is a composite of consequences for a system after the end of a crisis. The term refers to the degree of structural change or irreversibility and thus denotes the presence or absence of disequilibrium. The relationships among system components, crisis conditions, dimensions, and time are presented in Table 4.

TABLE 4

Conceptual Framework: System, Crisis and Change

System Components	Crisis Conditions	Dimension $(T_1)^*$	Dimension $(T_2)^*$
		SEVERITY+	IMPORTANCE+
INTERACTION	DISRUPTION	Actors	Power Change
		Involvement	Actor Change
		Geostrategy	Rules Change
		Heterogeneity	Alliance Change
		Issues	
		Violence	
STRUCTURE	INCIPIENT CHANGE		
	(in Power Distribution		
	Actor/Regimes		
	Rules		
	Alliances)		

$*T_1$ = during the crisis

$*T_2$ = after the crisis

+ Multiple indicators of Severity and Importance are ordered according to their relative weight; the rationale is set out in the presentation of the model below.

Severity and importance are mutually exclusive categories and are postulated as causally related: The overall severity of a crisis at its conclusion (Time T_1) predicts to its probable overall importance for an international system several years after the crisis has ended (T_2). Thus, knowledge about a configuration of severity during a future crisis should make it possible to anticipate its importance in world politics because a higher/lower level of severity is expected to produce more/less important changes in the structure of an international system.[15]

INDICATORS OF SEVERITY

The severity of an international crisis will be measured by six indicators: actors, involvement, geostrategy, heterogeneity, issues, and violence.[16] Each indicator will be defined in operational terms, with examples provided for the accompanying scale points.

Actors

The number of crisis actors in an international crisis is one indicator of its intensity: The participation of more actors signifies more widespread embryonic change during a crisis. There is considerable variation by actors among international crises from 1929 to 1979. They range from four celebrated cases with more than six crisis actors each (Entry into World War II, 21; Pearl Harbor, 10; Remilitarization of the Rhineland, 7; and Angola, 7) and several well-known crises with six actors (Israel Independence 1948-1949, Suez-Sinai Campaign 1956-1957, Berlin Wall 1961, Six Day War 1967, Prague Spring 1968) to many crises with the minimal number of one crisis actor.[17] The latter are found throughout the decades from the Chinese Eastern Railway Crisis in 1929 to the raid on Angola in 1979.

Cases also extend across the power hierarchy among states: superpowers (one or both) as crisis actors (Iran Hegemony 1945-1946, Berlin Blockade 1948-1949, Bay of Pigs 1961, Cuban Missiles 1962, Ussuri River 1969, War of Attrition 1969-1970, October–Yom Kippur War 1973-1974, Angola Crisis 1975-1976); major regional powers (India-China Border I and II, 1959-1960 and 1962, Egypt-Israel crises in 1948-1949, 1956-1957, 1960, 1967, 1969-1970, and 1973, and Bangladesh 1971); middle powers (Iran-Iraq crises over Shatt-al-Arab in 1959-1960, 1969, and 1980–present), and small powers as crisis actors (Pushtunistan I, II, and III, 1949-1950, 1955, and 1961-1962, between Afghanistan and Pakistan, Rwanda-Burundi 1963-1964, El

Salvador–Honduras Football War 1969). Cases with minimal crisis actor participation are found in most regions of the global system.

Involvement

Involvement refers to the extent of superpower or, in the 1930s, great power adversarial behavior in international crises. Clearly, superpower (SP) or great power confrontation as crisis actors indicates more intense disruption and incipient structural change than any other combination of their involvement in a crisis. Moreover, high involvement by the powers (direct or semi-military intervention or covert activity) signifies a greater potential structural change than low involvement (political or economic support for client states). And third, high involvement by both the United States and the USSR, or more than two great powers in the 1930s, indicates higher severity than a combination of high/low or high/no involvement—or even a combination of one major power as a crisis actor with others marginally or not involved; in the latter case the major power's adversarial role is muted and the systemic effects thereby lessened.

These assumptions generated a six-point scale of combinations of involvement by the superpowers in system crises: both SPs crisis actors (6); one SP a crisis actor, the other SP high involvement (5); both SPs high involvement (4); one SP a crisis actor, the other SP low or no involvement (3); one SP high involvement, the other SP low or no involvement (2); both SPs low or no involvement (1). A comparable six-point scale of involvement by the great powers was constructed for the period 1929 to 1945.

Illustrative cases can be found for every point on the superpower involvement scale. The 1973 October–Yom Kippur War was among the most severe (point 6) for this indicator: The U.S. nuclear alert in response to the Soviet threat of direct military intervention in Sinai was superimposed upon an intense confrontation between the major regional powers, Israel and Egypt-cum-Syria. A less severe combination is evident in the Guatemala Crisis of 1953-1954: The United States was a crisis actor, whereas the USSR was highly involved, dispatching military aid to its client, the Arbenz regime—an illustration of point 5 on this scale.

Both superpowers were highly involved—but neither was a crisis actor—in the 1964 Ethiopia-Somalia Crisis over Ogaden; the United States provided military aid to Ethiopia, the USSR to Somalia (point 4). The United States was a crisis actor in the Taiwan Straits Crisis of 1954-1955, supporting Taiwan, whereas USSR activity was confined to political support for the People's Republic of China (PRC), that is, low involvement. The extent of superpower involvement was reversed in the Prague Spring Crisis of 1968 (point 3). Illustrative of point 2 on the superpower involvement scale is the Catalina Affair in 1952: The USSR engaged in direct military activity, shooting down a Swedish flying boat, but U.S. involvement was minimal, restricted to verbal criticism of the Soviet act by the secretary of state. At the lowest point on the scale, the superpowers remained aloof in many crises, such as the 1951 Punjab War Scare between India and Pakistan and the extremely violent Rwanda-Burundi Crisis in 1963-1964.

Geostrategic Salience

Geostrategic salience, another indicator of crisis severity, refers to the location of a systemic crisis in terms of its natural resources, distance from major power centers, and so on. Geostrategic assets vary over time: Oil and uranium-producing regions acquired greater salience since the 1950s; coal-producing regions became less salient. Key waterways and choke points like Gibraltar, the Suez Canal, the Strait of Malacca, and the Panama Canal retained their geostrategic relevance over the decades. A combination of assets enhances geostrategic salience. For instance, the Strait of Hormuz provides access and egress from a region that, in the 1970s, produced 40 percent of the world's oil supply, with vast reserves to increase its geostrategic significance.

A broader geostrategic salience indicates more embryonic structural change during an international crisis. Moreover, a crisis located in a region of geostrategic interest to the dominant system, such as Central Europe since 1948 or the Arab-Israel conflict zone in the Middle East since 1956, will be more severe than one salient to a single subsystem (for example, South America or sub-Saharan Africa). At the same time, the direct participation of one or both superpowers, or prior to 1945 more than two great powers, in a systemic crisis does not per se indicate high geostrategic salience. The latter is determined by the significance of the location and resources of the crisis region for one or more international systems, not by the power of crisis actors. Geostrategic salience and extent of superpower/great power involvement tap two distinct though related components of overall crisis severity. Based upon these propositions a five-point scale was generated to score geostrategic relevance: relevant to the global system (5); to the dominant system and more than one subsystem (4); to the dominant system and one subsystem (3); to more than one subsystem (2); to and one subsystem (1).

Along with the Cuban Missile Crisis in 1962, the Middle East crises of 1956-1957 (Suez), 1967 (Six Day War) and 1973-1974 (October–

Yom Kippur War) score highest on this indicator of severity. For example, the oil embargo imposed by the Arab Gulf states in the Yom Kippur War had grave implications for Western Europe, Japan, and North America. Combined with the bottleneck in sea transportation created by the closure of the Suez Canal, it was geostrategically salient to the global system. All the Berlin crises (1948-1949, 1958-1959, 1961) were highly salient to the superpowers and the dominant system of world politics, as well as to the West European and East European subsystems, by virtue of their significance in the struggle for Germany, their symbolism for the future of Europe, and the centrality accorded these crises by both the United States and the USSR. The communism in Czechoslovakia Crisis in 1948 was salient to the dominant system and the USSR was a crisis actor, but the crisis was relevant to one subsystem only, Eastern Europe, and thus fell at point 3 on this scale. The India-China border crisis in 1962 impinged on South and East Asia but not on the dominant system of world politics. And at the lowest point of the geostrategy scale the crises over Pushtunistan in 1949, 1955, and 1961-1962 between Afghanistan and Pakistan were salient to one subsystem only, South Asia.

Heterogeneity

As for the extent of heterogeneity, severity is measured by the number, not the intensity, of attribute differences among adversaries. The attributes are military capability, economic development, political regime, and culture.

Every actor can be classified in terms of its military capability at the time of the crisis under inquiry. As noted, it will fall into one of four categories: super, major, middle, and small. For the period 1945-1979 only the United States and the USSR qualify as superpowers.[18] From 1929 to 1945 there were seven great powers: France (until 1940), Germany, the United Kingdom, Italy (until 1943), Japan, the Soviet Union, and the United States. With respect to military capability, heterogeneity is said to be present when any pair of adversarial actors in a systemic crisis belongs to more than one of the four levels of power.

Actors may also be classified in terms of economic development, as post-industrial, developed, and developing. Here too heterogeneity is regarded as present when adversaries are identified with more than one level of development (North Vietnam and the United States in many Indo-China crises) and as absent when the adversaries are at the same level of development (Ethiopia and Somalia in all of their crises over the Ogaden).

Heterogeneity also includes political regime, which is classified as democratic, civil authoritarian, military, and dual authority. This element is evident in all crises between Nazi Germany and democratic Britain and France from 1933 to 1945, all U.S.-USSR crises, many India-Pakistan crises, and almost all Arab-Israel crises. It is absent in most intra-African crises because of widespread presence of military regimes. There may also be heterogeneity with respect to the cultural attribute, referring to belief systems, ideologies, languages, and so on.

More attribute differences among adversaries in an international crisis indicate more cleavages and, therefore, greater severity.[19] Thus the values for this indicator are scored in ascending order from no heterogeneity, point 1, to total heterogeneity, that is, differences in all four attributes, point 5. In cases where the extent of heterogeneity varies among adversarial pairs, the most heterogeneous pair is used for this indicator, for example, the United States and North Korea, not the two Koreas, in the Korean War Crisis 1950-1951.

Maximal heterogeneity among crisis adversaries is evident in the 1956-1957 Suez case. The United Kingdom and France were major powers in global terms, and Egypt was at most a middle power, though a major power in the Middle East. The former countries were economically advanced; the latter had a very poor developing economy. The adversaries differed in political regime—Western democracy versus military authoritarianism—and in culture—language, belief system, and so on. These differences were accentuated because the United Kingdom and France were struggling to preserve existing international system rules regarding rights embodied in interstate agreements over the Suez Canal whereas Egypt was asserting national rights as the basis of a higher rule.

In the Trieste Crisis of 1953 Italy and Yugoslavia differed on all but one attribute of heterogeneity: an economically developed versus a developing economy; a Western democracy versus a Communist political regime; and cultural differences embracing language, religion, and history. In terms of military capability both states were middle powers; thus this case is scored 4 on the scale of heterogeneity.

The 1947 Marshall Plan Crisis illustrates adversary differences in two attributes: political—Western democracy versus a Soviet regime; and military—a small power versus a superpower. The two crisis actors, Czechoslovakia and the USSR, were more akin than different in culture and level of economic development, leading to a score of 3 for heterogeneity.

One attribute differed between India and Pakistan in their post-partition crises over Junagadh, Kashmir, and Hyderabad in 1947–

1949. India was primarily influenced by Hindu culture, Pakistan by Islam; hence a score of 2 on the heterogeneity scale. The lowest point on this scale is illustrated by the 1959-1960 crisis ensuing from Cuba-inspired invasions of several Caribbean and Central American states. The adversaries were all small powers, with underdeveloped economies, authoritarian regimes, and an inheritance of Spanish-American culture. Moreover, intervention in the affairs of neighbors by support for mercenaries or more direct means was an established practice in inter-American relations, though without legal sanction.

Issues

Issues can be defined at three levels: case, cluster, and area. A case issue indicates the focus of a specific crisis for a state, such as the control over governmental power in Czechoslovakia's 1948 crisis with the Soviet Union. A cluster issue refers to the common theme among related cases, for example, Soviet hegemony in East European crises from 1945 to 1949. Issue-area denotes generic substance, that is, groups of clusters of issues with a shared focus. These clusters can be grouped into four issue-areas: (a) military-security, incorporating territories, borders, free navigation, change in military balance, military incidents, and war; (b) political-diplomatic, including sovereignty, hegemony, and international influence; (c) economic-developmental, including the nationalization of property, raw materials, economic pressure such as boycotts and sanctions, and foreign exchange problems; and (d) cultural-status, comprising issues of ideology, challenge to nonmaterial values, symbols.

A crisis over a military-security issue alone indicates more severity than a crisis concerned with any other issue-area. Moreover, crises involving multiple issues identify more incipient structural change than those dealing with a single issue. Five points on an issue scale of severity have been generated: three or more issues (5); two issues, including military-security (4); a military-security issue alone (3); two issues other than military-security (2); one nonmilitary issue (1).

Some international crises are concerned with a single issue: It may be political, as in the 1958 Formation of the United Arab Republic (UAR), which posed a challenge to the existing regimes in Iraq and Jordan; it may be economic, as in the Jordan Waters case in 1963-1964, involving Israel and its immediate neighbors, Egypt, Jordan, Lebanon, and Syria. Both of these crises have the lowest score on the issue scale. More often a military issue alone is the concern, as in the 1964 Ethiopia-Somalia Crisis over the territory of Ogaden. An illustration of two issues other than military-security is provided by the 1965 Dominican Republic Crisis, which had political and status implications. The most frequent type of crisis is one involving military-security and another issue-area, point 4 on this scale. For example, in the 1967 Cyprus Crisis both territory and influence in the eastern Mediterranean were issues between Greece and Turkey. Less common are three-issue crises such as the 1961 Berlin Wall case, which combined future control over a visible pro-Western outpost in the Communist part of Europe, the credibility of the superpowers with allies and adversaries alike, and the status of communism in East Germany and East Europe generally as a viable political-economic system.

Violence

The extent of violence in an international crisis is the last indicator of its severity. Clearly, hostile physical acts in a crisis are more severe than hostile verbal interaction. Moreover, violence is more disruptive than any other method of crisis management. A four-point scale ascends from no violence (1), through minor clashes resulting in few or no casualties (2), to limited violence, that is, serious clashes short of war (3), to full-scale war (4).

War occurs frequently in international crises, as in Korea 1950–1953, the Middle East crises of 1948-1949, 1956-1957, 1967, 1969-1970, and 1973-1974, the 1969 Football War, the 1971 Bangladesh Crisis, and Cyprus in 1974. Even more frequent are serious clashes short of war, as in the 1969 Ussuri River Crisis between the PRC and the USSR and the Taiwan Straits Crises of 1954-1955 and 1958. Minor clashes, too, occurred in many crises, such as Costa Rica–Nicaragua in 1948-1949 and the Iceland–United Kingdom Cod War in 1973. Celebrated illustrations of crises with no violence are the Berlin crises of 1948-1949, 1957–1959 and 1961.

INDICATORS OF IMPORTANCE

The importance of an international crisis will be measured by four indicators[20] of system change: change in power distribution, actors, rules of the game, and alliance configuration. These indicators are derived from the definition of a crisis, notably from the condition of actual change in the structure of a system. Ordinal scales for each indicator, along with empirical illustrations from the data set, will now be specified.

Distribution of Power

Effects on the distribution of power within an international system refer to change in both the number of power centers and the hierarchy of power. A scale for this indicator of importance encompasses change in the composition of states at the apex of a power pyramid (4), in the ranking of states among the five most powerful within the dominant subsystem (3), and in the relative power of adversarial crisis actors (2), and includes instances in which no change in relative power occurs among adveraries (1).[21] A measurement of these shifts is based upon two assumptions: first, that change in the composition of the apex group is of greater consequence for an international system than change of rank within the top five or among less powerful states; and second, that changes in rank outweigh changes in short-term power distribution between adversaries after the conclusion of a crisis.

Changes in the composition of the power elite within an international system are rare. Japan is a notable example of a country that exited from the most powerful group as a consequence of the Atomic Bomb Intra-War Crisis in August 1945. The People's Republic of China entered into this exclusive club following its triumph in the China Civil War of 1948-1949. The crisis attending the formation of the United Arab Republic (UAR) in 1958 provides an example of a change in rank; Egypt re-emerged as the most powerful state in the Middle East Subsystem, point 3 on the change-in-power scale.

In the 1956 Hungarian Crisis the USSR and its Warsaw Pact allies perceived victory whereas Hungary considered the outcome a defeat; however, there was no shift in the power hierarchy within the Soviet bloc. In the Cuban Missile Crisis the United States perceived victory and the USSR defeat, as did Cuba, but there was no change in power rank between the superpowers. Finally, at the lowest point, there was no change in relative power among adversarial crisis actors in many international crises since World War II, such as those in Trieste in 1953, in Taiwan Straits in 1958, in Algeria-Morocco in 1963, in Rwanda-Burundi in 1963-1964, in India-Pakistan in 1965-1966, and on Ussuri River in 1969.

Actors

Change in actors comprises both regime change, whether in orientation or type, and a more basic structural shift, namely, the emergence, preservation, or disappearance of one or more independent states as a result of an international crisis. This change is expressed in a four-point scale: creation/preservation/elimination of one or more state actors (4); change in regime type (3); change in regime orientation (2); no change in actors or regime (1).

One example of basic actor change was the creation of a new state, Bangladesh, as a result of the 1971 India-Pakistan Crisis. Another was the extinction of South Vietnam through merger with North Vietnam following the termination of the Vietnam systemic crisis in 1975. An illustration of a change in regime type was the replacement of a democratic government in Prague by a Communist regime as a consequence of the 1947-1948 Czechoslovakia crisis. Similarly, the regime of Prince Sihanouk gave way to a military group headed by Lon Noe following the 1970 Cambodia Crisis. As for a shift in foreign policy orientation, the Guatemala Crisis in 1953-1954 led from a pro-Soviet to a pro-U.S. regime in that state. So too did the 1973-1974 October–Yom Kippur Crisis, with Sadat initiating the Arab-Israeli peace process three years later. The majority of systemic crises between 1929 and 1979 did not produce a change in the number of actors or in the type or policy of regimes.

Rules of the Game

The rules of the game are those norms derived from law, custom, morality, or self-interest that serve as guidelines for legitimate behavior by the actors of a system. These rules may be informal or formally codified. They may be violated frequently. However, they remain valid as long as states persist in acknowledging their legitimacy and act so as to avoid the stigma of violating these norms. Even when actors initiate violence they invariably invoke the right of self-defense. Given this pattern of behavior (acknowledging the legitimating role of norms), rules of the game can be said to change very slowly. Changes in rules include a change in the content of existing rules; the creation or elimination of rules; and a modification in actor consensus about a system's rules of behavior.

These changes can be measured on the basis of two assumptions. First, the institutionalization of rules of the game involves a more extended process in time than the emergence of consensus about informal norms of behavior; thus changes in institutionalized rules are more significant for the long-term functioning of an international system. It is also assumed that a change in content follows a shift in the extent of consensus rather than the reverse, and "dissensus," in turn, leads to a change in permissable rules of behavior. For example, codified rules on prisoners of war traditionally exclude terrorists from this status; however, a declining consensus is evident in the late 1970s and early 1980s that may eventually result in a rule change that in effect legitimizes terrorism.

These considerations lead to a four-point scale. The creation or elimination of codified or tacit rules of the game in the context of an international crisis (point 4) occurs infrequently. A noteworthy example is the Brezhnev Doctrine in the 1968 Prague Spring Crisis: Then and subsequently East European interstate relations were to be guided by the higher principle of Soviet bloc interests instead of the time-honored principles of state sovereignty and nonintervention. An illustration of point 3 regarding changes in rules of the game was the breakdown of the consensus over the status and governance of Berlin, as evident in the cumulative crises of 1948-1949 (blockade), 1958-1959 (deadline), and 1961 (wall). The decline in consensus about tacit rules (point 2) is evident in the use of paratroops by the United States and Belgium to protect Westerners in Stanleyville during the 1964 Congo Crisis, a precedent for future behavior in such abnormal crisis conditions. Most crises, however, have no visible effect on rules of the game (point 1), whether informal or institutionalized.

Alliance Configuration

Change in Alliance Configuration means shifts in the structure or functioning of alliances within an international system. These include the formation or elimination of an alliance or changes within an existing alliance—in the number of actors and the extent of cohesiveness. Two assumptions underlie a scale to measure these systemic changes: First, a change in the number of alliances will have more far-reaching effects on an international system than change within an existing alliance: and second, among alliance attributes change in the number of members will have the greatest impact. Alliance shifts are measured along a four-point ordinal scale: formation/elimination of an alliance (4); entry/exit of actor(s) into/from a formal or informal alliance (3); increase/decrease of cohesiveness within an existing alliance (2); no change in alliance configuration (1).

There are few illustrations of the formation or elimination of an alliance as a consequence of an international crisis. The Sino-Soviet Alliance of 1950 following the China Civil War is one. Another is the creation of an informal Egypt-United States alliance in the aftermath of the 1973-1974 Middle East Crisis. The 1970 Cambodia Crisis led to that country's entry into a U.S.-led alliance engaged in a war against North Vietnam. One effect of the 1968 Prague Spring Crisis was increasing cohesiveness among Warsaw Pact countries. Typical cases in which no change occurred in alliance configuration were the crises in Trieste in 1953 and Mayaguez in 1975.

THE LOGIC OF INDICES

The central postulate of the Crisis-as-Earthquake Model is that the importance of an international crisis is primarily a product of its

FIGURE 2   <u>Crisis-as-Earthquake Model</u>

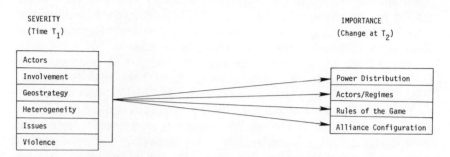

The independent/dependent variables are listed in order of weight, according to the scope of their spillover effects. These will be addressed in the construction of the Index of Severity and the Index of Importance.

severity. In other words, the extent of disequilibrium resulting from a systemic crisis is expected to depend on the degree of instability that it has generated.[22] Importance refers to the impact of a crisis on the structure of an international system or its significance as a catalyst to system change after the termination of a crisis (T_2). Severity, as noted, refers to the intensity of a crisis or the extent of disruptive interaction and incipient structural dislocation during the life-span of the crisis (T_1) (see Figure 2).

In model terms, the relationship of severity to importance is that of composite independent variable to composite dependent variable. The indicators of severity have been specified as the number of actors; the extent of superpower involvement; the scope of the geostrategic salience of the crisis; the extent of heterogeneity among the adversaries; the issues in dispute; and the level of violence. The indicators of importance are change in power distribution, actors/regimes, rules of the game, and alliance configuration.

The model postulates that severity explains importance. The most general hypothesis, therefore, can be formulated as follows:

The higher the severity of an international crisis, that is, the larger the number of crisis actors, the more actively involved the superpowers/ major powers, the broader the scope of geostrategic salience, the more heterogeneous the adversaries, the wider the range of disputed issues, and the more serious the violence, *the greater will be the importance of a crisis,* that is, the greater will be the extent of system change, whether a shift in the distribution of power, the creation/elimination of an actor or change in regime type or orientation, change in the rules of the game, or change in the pattern of alliances—change in one or more of these structural attributes of an international system.

Within this overarching hypothesis are nested many narrow-gauge hypotheses linking one or more severity attributes to one or more importance attributes because the six indicators of severity constitute interrelated independent variables and the four indicators of importance are the interrelated dependent variables that together constitute system change. Illustrations of the 24 potential bivariate linkages include the following:

1. The larger the number of adversarial actors in an international crisis, the greater the shift in the postcrisis pattern of alliances.
2. The more heterogeneous the crisis actors, the more will systemic rules of the game be undermined and the more durable the change after the crisis.

There are also many multivariate linkages that can be hypothesized between severity and importance attributes. For example,

3. The broader the geostrategic salience of a crisis, the greater the changes in rules of the game and in the alliance pattern of an international system.
4. The wider the range of disputed issues and the greater the heterogeneity among the adversaries, the more extensive the crosscutting effects on existing alliances and consequent shifts in the post-crisis alliance configuration.
5. The higher the level of violence in a crisis, the more far-reaching change in actors or regimes and in the redistribution of power within an international system after the termination of the crisis.

These and other specific hypotheses, which derive from the Crisis-as-Earthquake Model, will not be tested in this book. Rather, the focus will be on the general link between the intensity of a crisis at T_1 and the extent of its consequences for a system at T_2. Thus it is hypothesized that the scores for overall severity and overall importance will be highly correlated.

The core task in operationalizing the model is to determine the relative weight of the independent and dependent variables in overall severity and overall importance, respectively. This determination requires the construction of an Index of Severity and an Index of Importance that can be used to generate comparable scores for, and a rank order of, international crises along these two dimensions. The findings will provide a test of the model's validity and the accuracy of its overarching hypothesis. This test, in turn, will permit an assessment of the efficacy of the proposed method of forecasting the likely impact of future international crises as catalysts to system change.

Index of Severity

The Index of Severity is based upon a weighted summation of the indicators. By specifying their potential impact on the structure of an international system, these weights will be derived deductively. An alternative approach would be to obtain weights through an inductive method such as factor analysis. The deductive strategy has been adopted to preserve the logical consistency of the general investigation of systemic crisis and its role in catalyzing change. Causal inferences about severity and importance are at issue, not the statistical associations among indicators. M. Friedman has developed this argument at greater length, although his context is somewhat different:

> The relevant question to ask about the "assumptions" of a theory is not whether they are descriptively "realistic," for they never are, but whether they are sufficiently good approximations for the purpose at hand. And this question can be answered only by seeing whether the theory works, which means whether it yields sufficiently accurate predictions. The two supposedly independent tests thus reduce to one test. (1953: 15)

The purpose at hand is the prediction of importance on the basis of severity. This relation is hypothesized to be one of cause and effect. All other things being equal, an index based on the presumed cause-and-effect relations among its constituents has more theoretical value than one obtained through an inductive technique. This is true for both severity and importance, because the structure of each index can be understood in logical, as opposed to statistical, terms. Accordingly, the initial attempt to construct indices will be deductive: The weight of each indicator will be derived from its presumed causal linkages and its spillover effects on the other indicators. Subsequent predictive performance then can be used to argue for (or against) the use of an alternative, inductive approach to the generation of indices.

Since there are six indicators of severity, and each conceivably could be related in a causal manner to any (or all) of the others, there exists a maximum of 30 potential linkages.[23] As noted, the weight assigned to each indicator will be based on the number of linkages it is expected to have with the others and thus its input into overall severity.[24] The linkages are presented in composite form in the center of Figure 3 and individually in Figures 3A-F, surrounding the center.

Actors. For actors (indicator s_1), four linkages are postulated (Figure 3A), and one indicator is independent of its effects. Geostrategic salience is an a priori attribute of a given region. For example, the level of significance attributed to the Middle East as a crisis region is based on characteristics such as resource assets and does not rise or fall with the number of actors involved in a crisis there. As an inherent characteristic of a region, geostrategic salience in fact is independent of the other indicators as well. Thus, in the summary of linkages the potential effects of other indicators on geostrategic relevance will not be discussed.

The number of actors (N) is expected to affect heterogeneity: a larger N necessarily increases the size of the set of paired comparisons between crisis actors that can be made. The number of dyads is a quadratic function of the number of crisis actors.[25] When there are more dyads there also exist more opportunities for comparing the actors concerned and, potentially, for finding highly disparate pairs. Consequently, heterogeneity by and large is expected to be greater in large groups.

Involvement too is considered to be sensitive to the number of actors. A larger number of participants makes a given international crisis more pervasive to the system. As such, the likelihood of superpower involvement is expected to be higher because the Soviet Union and United States will be more concerned with crises that may introduce fundamental changes to the system. Essentially this proposition rests on the assumption that the superpowers will tend to act as system-managers.

Also linked positively to the number of actors is the range of issues in a crisis. A more extensive set of participants has a greater potential to produce different coalition structures. And the more complex coalitional possibilities that result from the entry of new actors will facilitate the linking of issues currently operative in a crisis to others that, until that point, had remained latent. In other words, as the size of the group involved in a crisis increases so too does the potential scope of bargaining.

Actors may also affect the resort to violence. As a general rule, when a large number of parties is involved in a bargaining sequence it is more difficult to obtain a solution that will satisfy all concerned. Thus, under such circumstances there is reason to expect that one (or more) actors will resort to violent means to obtain their objectives.

Superpower Involvement. Superpower involvement (indicator s_2) is also linked to four other indicators of severity (Figure 3B). When the

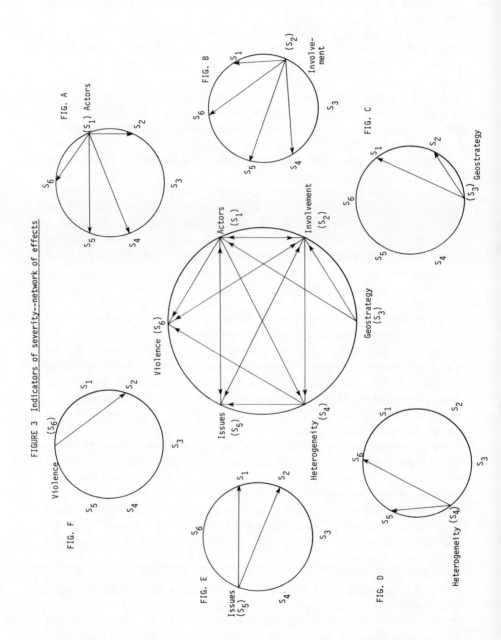

FIGURE 3 Indicators of severity—network of effects

United States or USSR is active in a crisis this participation is expected to lead to involvement by other actors as well; that is, the actions of a superpower will more readily result in spillover into the international system. More generally, the behavior of a superpower in a given realm has greater implications for developments elsewhere. For example, when a superpower issues a threat, it may be salient to members of the international polity other than the immediate target.

It is obvious intuitively why greater heterogeneity will result from superpower involvement. The superpowers are qualitatively different from the rest of the members of the international polity. When one of these giants is involved in a crisis, it is almost certain that at least one rather disparate dyad will result from the process of pairwise comparison. Thus superpower involvement has the effect of raising the probable level of diversity among actors in a crisis setting.

Superpowers have global interests. When they become active in a crisis the range of issues in that crisis may expand. As a result of their panoramic concerns, superpowers can introduce new issues to a bargaining process—issues that might otherwise have been left out altogether.

There is reason to expect a lower level of violence when superpowers are involved in crises. At the systemic level there are certain behavioral norms with regard to superpower behavior. The United States and USSR have capabilities that dwarf those even of other nuclear powers. Thus, their use of violence is expected by system members (and especially each other) to be calibrated carefully with the importance of a conflict because of the ever-present danger of miscalculation and escalation to the nuclear level.[26]

Geostrategy. Geostrategy (indicator s_3) is expected to have an impact on two other severity indicators whereas the remaining three are independent of its effects (Figure 3C). The geostrategic salience of a crisis is likely to affect the number of states that ultimately become crisis actors. If absolute distance is held constant, the probability that a state will become involved in a given crisis will increase with the perceived significance of the region in which the crisis occurs.

Crises in locations of high geostrategic salience are more likely to induce superpower activity. The basis for this inference is twofold. The United States and USSR are less sensitive than other states to the costs attendant upon involvement in distant crises; a crisis in a significant setting may trigger superpower involvement even if it is at a great physical distance.[27] Moreover, the previously mentioned concerns for system management are expected to lead to a high level of superpower involvement in crises that occur in strategic settings.[28]

Heterogeneity. Heterogeneity (indicator s_4) is expected to affect two other indicators of severity (Figure 3D). There is good reason to assume that it will have a direct impact on the range of issues. Disparity increases the probability that parties to a crisis will possess different images of their bargaining environment. Consequently, some actors may try to link new issues to those already under consideration. As a general rule, this will tend to increase the range of issues ultimately raised by crisis participants.

Heterogeneity is also expected to lead to a higher level of violence. Members of a diverse group, even if rather small, may experience problems in coordinating their behavior, a challenge that would not confront more homogeneous groups. Failure by them to communicate intentions through subtle means could cause some participants to act violently. In other words, violent crisis management techniques are expected to occur as a result of misperception among members of heterogeneous groups.[29]

Issues. Issues (indicator s_5) also have an effect upon two other indicators of severity (Figure 3E). As the range of issues increases so will the set of actors drawn into a crisis; a further topic for bargaining may elicit the entry of one or more additional actors, who may have been indifferent to previous points of contention. Moreover, a large number of issues increases the probability of inducing the participation of a given actor. This, in turn, will increase heterogeneity, an indirect link.

Superpower involvement also is in part a function of the range of issues. Multiple-issue crises have the potential to produce change in more than one facet of international relations. Given their system-wide concerns, the superpowers can be expected to become involved in interactions that potentially have more general implications for the international polity.[30]

Violence. Violence (indicator s_6) is expected to affect only one other indicator of severity—superpower involvement (Figure 3F). Crises that have escalated to military confrontation must be viewed as intense. As such, they are likely to gain the attention of one superpower, perhaps both, because of the far-reaching interests of the United States and USSR. The superpowers will become concerned with violent crises especially because these are disruptive interactions that have the potential to produce fundamental and long-term changes for their participants and for the system as a whole.[31]

This completes the deductive derivation of linkages among severity indicators. It is now possible to assign values to the weights: w_1 (actors) = 4; w_2 (involvement) = 4; w_3 (geostrategy) = 2; w_4 (heterogeneity) = 2; w_5 (issues) = 2; and w_6 (violence) = 1.

Index of Importance

The Index of Importance consists of a weighted summation of its indicators. As in the case of the Severity Index, these weights will be arrived at deductively through an assessment of the potential linkages. Since there are four indicators, there is a maximum of twelve possible linkages. The weight assigned to a given indicator is based on the number of linkages expected with the others.[32] The center of Figure 4 presents the entire set of linkages, which are broken down individually in the side circles.

Power Distribution. Change in power distribution (indicator i_1) affects each of the other indicators of importance (Figure 4A). When the concentration of power in an international system changes, so does the extent of autonomy of its members. If power becomes more dispersed, the actors may be in a better position to pursue active or even aggressive policies. If, by contrast, the system becomes more stratified, the role of individual states may be restricted. In sum, shifting power distributions have implications for the foreign policy orientations of states.

Alliance configuration, too, is sensitive to the changing distribution of power. Although ideology is also an important factor, coalitional dynamics usually reflect changes in the dispersion of capabilities among system members. Alliances, which provide security for those who in isolation might see themselves as vulnerable, undergo change as the power constellation and consequent perceived threat changes.

Although rules of the game evolve gradually, changes in the distribution of capabilities have more influence on them than do other kinds of structural change. In an atomistic society such as the international polity, the law generally will reflect the preferences of actors capable of reacting decisively to perceived violations. Although even the most powerful actors face some constraints, knowledge of the power hierarchy in the system or one of its subsystems will tell a great deal about how rights and rules are likely to be interpreted in a given case.

Actors. From Figure 4B it is apparent that a change in actors (indicator i_2) is expected to affect two other indicators. A change in the number or kind of actors is likely to have an impact on the existing alliance configuration. If an actor exists from (or enters into) a given subsystem, it affects the calculations made by the other actors who must interact within that environment. Thus changes in actors may destabilize or solidify existing coalitional arrangements, since alliances are used by states to ameliorate the ever-present security dilemma.

52

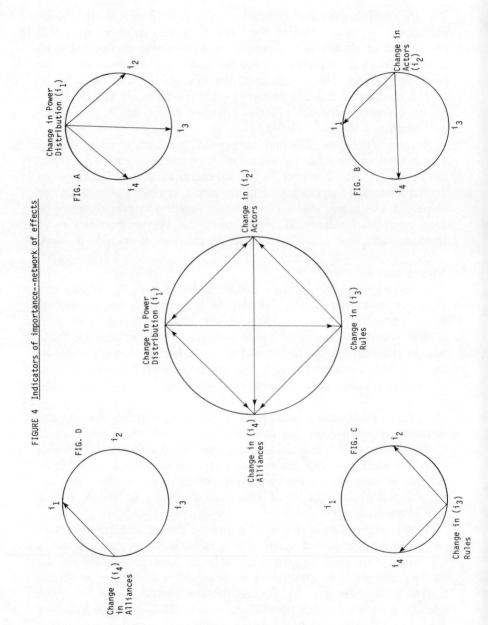

FIGURE 4 Indicators of importance--network of effects

Power distribution, too, is expected to be responsive to changes in actors. Certainly the deletion of an actor from, or addition to, a subsystem will affect the distribution of power in that milieu. A new regime for one or more of the actors could also have an impact because the values and intentions of the elite of that state could differ significantly from those of its predecessor. Thus both quantitative and qualitative changes in actors have implications for the distribution of power.[33]

Rules of the Game. Change in rules of the game (indicator i_3) affects two other indicators of importance (Figure 4C). Prevailing norms will have a definite impact on the conduct of actors at the international level. As these norms evolve so too will the beliefs held by elites about what constitutes permissable foreign policy behavior.

Alliances also will be sensitive to rule changes. Like an individual state the actor in an alliance will be concerned about the boundaries of legitimate conduct in the system, although such laws are not always obeyed strictly. Rule changes may make an alliance more (or less) attractive to one (or more) of its members. Evolving rules also can catalyze the formation of new alliances in response to newly perceived problems. Rule changes affect the way actual and potential alliance partners perceive their objectives, and hence the rules of the game are likely to have an impact on alliance dynamics.[34]

Alliances. Change in alliances (indicator i_4) affects only one other indicator of importance, the distribution of power (Figure 4D). This expectation is based upon the assumption that there are returns to scale for alliance partners. More simply, if an existing alliance collapses or a new one is formed, this change will have implications for the capacity of states in those coalitions to act in a coordinated manner. This assumption will be true to a lesser degree when an existing alliance becomes more or less cohesive.[35]

This completes the analysis of linkages for the Importance Index. The weights for its components are u_1 (power change) = 3; u_2 (actor change) = 2; u_3 (rules change) = 2; and u_4 (alliance change) = 1.

Unlike the dimension of severity, which is confined to the duration of a crisis per se, importance is assessed for a time period beyond the conclusion of a crisis. This period is necessarily set arbitrarily. However, certain considerations guided our choice of a three-year period after the termination of a crisis. Given the nature of systemic changes, a shorter time would not permit them to unfold. This is especially true for the rules of the game; changes in this area may be imperceptible unless measured in years. By contrast, if a longer period were selected, the competing effects of diverse crises and other international phenomena could not be readily disentangled. The three-year period will not be applied rigidly. In those rare cases in which a structural change became manifest more than three years after the termination of a systemic crisis (but was latent within the system prior to the "deadline"), it will be incorporated in the coding. A striking illustration is the fundamental change in the rules of the game within the Middle East subsystem symbolized by Anwar Sadat's journey to Jerusalem in November 1977, three and a half years after the end of the 1973-1974 October–Yom Kippur Crisis.

3

Findings

The empirical results of this study will be presented in several stages. First, a descriptive analysis of the data will be provided through a system and geographic distribution for the scale points of the indicators of severity.[36] Second, the indicators of severity and importance will be correlated within each index. These exercises are intended to demonstrate that the indices are streamlined and valid, a prerequisite to any analyses that include either overall severity or importance. Third, the overall severity of all 278 crises from 1929 to 1979 will be examined in different system-periods and geographic regions. Fourth, the top 10 percent of the data set along the dimension of severity will be isolated for intensive study. Consisting of 26 cases at the apex of severity, the subset to be examined obviously in interesting (and manageable) for purposes of comparison. This stage of the analysis will describe the distribution of cases in terms of geography, system-period, power discrepancy, and each of the six components of severity. Thereafter the link between severity and importance for this subset of crises is discussed. This is followed by in-depth discussion of two case studies of severity and importance, the Middle East Crisis, 1973-1974, and the Angola Crisis, 1975-1976. The final stage of the analysis will concern findings in the aggregate. A contingency table and ordinary least squares (OLS) regression will be used to test the predictive power of severity with respect to importance.

SEVERITY DATA: A DESCRIPTIVE ANALYSIS

Actors

The distribution of the number of crisis actors by system-period and geography/space is set out in Tables 5 and 6. For the 50-year period as a whole there was a single crisis actor in 107 cases (38.5 percent), and one or two crisis actors in 214 (77 percent) of the 278 international crises. The frequency of cases diminishes as actor participation increases; that is, the proportion of cases with three to five or more crisis actors shows a steady decline from 9.7 percent to 6.1 percent.

There was a relatively equal proportional share of single-actor and two-actor cases in the multipolar, bipolar, and polycentric systems; only World War II, surprisingly, shows a high concentration (54.8 percent) of single-actor crises. This observation probably results from the prevalence of a powerful adversary initiating—but not perceiving—a crisis (e.g., Germany vis-à-vis weaker European states; the United States vis-à-vis Japan in the latter's intra-war crises in 1944-1945). As for the multiple-actor categories, the proportions are consistent across the different system-periods.

The largest concentration of one- and two-actor cases, by region, occurred in the Americas, with 90.9 percent, followed by Africa (84.4 percent), and Asia (82.6 percent), with the Middle East (69.1 percent), somewhat below the overall average for the entire set of crises—77.0 percent—and Europe (61.4 percent) well below the average. As for the multiple-actor cases, Europe accounted for more than one-third of all crises with three or more actors, 22 of 64 cases, followed by the Middle East, with 17 or 64 cases, most of which were crises between Israel and two or more Arab states. At the upper level of number of crisis actors, Europe and the Middle East were the locations of 8 and 5, respectively, of the 17 cases with five or more actors.

Superpower Involvement

The distribution of adversarial great power/superpower involvement in crises, by system-period and geography/space, is set out in Tables 7–10. Although the involvement categories for the pre- and post-1945 international systems are not identical and not strictly comparable, they can be compared in terms of broad clusters of high involvement (first three rows) and high and low involvement (last three rows), as well as at the extremes of involvement. Since the World War II cases stand apart from all others, with 61.2 percent high involvement by powers as adversaries, compared to 23.7 percent for the 1930s cases and 13.9 percent for post-1945 cases, they are not included in the analysis by systems.

The central points that can be seen in Tables 7 and 8 are (1) the absence of high adversarial involvement by the powers in crises for the 50-year period as a whole, except for the World War II cases, which, because of the weight accorded to involvement in the Index of Severity raises the overall severity of the 1939–1945 crises (see Table 24); and (2) the steady increase of low or no involvement from the multipolar to the bipolar to the polycentric systems. At the upper end of the involvement spectrum, adversarial superpower involvement in the multipolar system was the highest (7.9 percent) as expected, compared to 7.5 percent in the bipolar system and 3.4 percent in the polycentric system. At the lower end of the involvement spectrum, both SPs were uninvolved or little involved in 56.9 percent of all post-1945 crises, more so in the polycentric than in the bipolar system; that is, they did not usually seek to exploit international turbulence to enhance their own influence. Noninvolvement or low involvement by the great powers in the 1930s was much less conspicuous, 34.2 percent, indicating a more active role in crises.

In terms of regions (Tables 9 and 10), minimal adversarial involvement by the great powers in crises within the multipolar system of the 1930s was prevalent in 87.5 percent of Americas' crises and modest in crises within Europe and the Middle East. Low involvement of the great powers (the first three categories of Table 9 combined) was characteristic of all crises in the Americas and the Middle East and almost all in Africa.

The comparable figures for the bipolar and polycentric system together (crises from 1945 to 1979) are as follows: Minimal involvement (category 1 in Table 10) was very prominent in Africa (79.7 percent), followed by the Middle East (59.2 percent), and the Americas (56.0 percent); and low involvement (the first three categories combined) ranged from 81.7 percent in the Middle East to 88.2 percent in Africa. In short, superpower adversarial involvement in crises from 1945 to 1979 was much less conspicuous than great power adversarial involvement in crises of the 1930s.

The most frequent type of adversarial involvement within each region was as follows:

Asia	(1929–1945)	One great power as a crisis actor, the others high or low involvement
	(1945–1979)	Both superpowers, the others low or no involvement
Europe	(1929–1945)	
	(1945–1979)	Same as Asia
Americas	(1929–1945)	Two or more great powers low or no involvement
	(1945–1979)	Both superpowers low or no involvement
Middle East	(1929–1945)	One or two great powers as crisis actors, the others low involvement
	(1945–1979)	Same as the Americas

Africa   (1929–1945)   Same as Middle East
                (1945–1979)   Same as the Americas

Geostrategy

The distribution of geostrategic salience by system and geography is set out in Tables 11 and 12. For the 50-year period as a whole, more than one-half of the 278 international crises (57.9 percent) were characterized by minimal geostrategic salience, that is, to one subsystem only. The distribution in terms of system levels, namely, relevance to subsystem(s) or dominant-global system(s), was 70.5 percent and 29.5 percent, respectively.

Comparison across system-periods reveals that a large majority of crises in the polycentric system (74.1 percent) was salient to a single subsystem; this reflects the enormous increase since 1945 of small, weak actors in Africa and Asia, whose foreign policy behavior was of little relevance to the superpower-led dominant international system and the broader global system. Yet in both the multipolar and bipolar systems half or more of the crises had minimal salience; the 57.9 percent in the former is surprising, in the light of many 1930s crises in the European dominant system initiated by Germany, but this category also includes all Sino-Japanese (East Asia only) cases during that decade. And the 35.5 percent for dominant plus subsystem reflects the European cases during World War II. Only the bipolar system was characterized by a substantial block (23.7 percent) of cases that were relevant to two or more regional subsystems. As expected, most World War II crises (71.0 percent) had a much broader geostrategic salience.

The distribution of cases among the three categories of dominant and global systems was relatively equal in the bipolar and polycentric systems. The proportion of multipolar cases that were salient to the dominant system was much higher than in the post–World War II systems, 36.8 percent, compared to 26.8 percent (bipolar) and 18.1 percent (polycentric). This result reflects the smaller number of actors before World War II; the proportion of the actors that were members of the great power dominant system in the 1930s was higher than that of actors after 1945 that were members of the superpower-led dominant system. Finally, World War II accounted for 7 of the 12 cases with maximal geostrategic salience.

As evident in Table 12, the vast majority of crises in the Americas, Africa, and the Middle East were salient to subsystems only—90.9 percent, 89.1 percent, and 78.2 percent, respectively. The percentage for Asia was somewhat lower (66.7 percent). At the other extreme was Europe with 35.1 percent of its crises relevant to the subsystem level only.

At the level of dominant system cum global system, Europe, mainly because of the concentration of World War II cases, accounted for the largest proportion, 37 of 82 cases, or 45.1 percent, followed by Asia and the Middle East, 23 or 82, or 28.4 percent, and 12 of 82, or 14.6 percent, respectively, at that level. Africa was the only region without a crisis salient to the entire global system.

Heterogeneity

Tables 13 and 14 indicate the distribution of heterogeneity between pairs of adversarial actors, by system and geography. For the 50-year period as a whole, there were relatively few international crises with either no attribute differences between adversaries (9.7 percent) or one such difference (10.8 percent). One-third of all crises (33.5 percent) had all four attribute differences, that is, maximal heterogeneity, followed by cases with two (24.5 percent), then three (21.6 percent), attribute differences. This distribution may result from a link between successful negotiation of disputes, without escalation to crises, and a high degree of homogeneity between adversaries; in other words, states with relatively equal military and economic power and/or that have a common culture and/or political system find it easier—and in their interests—to negotiate differences with other states rather than risk the potentially high costs of crises.

Virtually the same distribution of cases with two or three attribute differences is evident in all three system-periods other than that for World War II. In terms of region, the Americas stand apart from the high concentration of crises with little heterogeneity; 60.6 percent of all cases in that region showed no attribute difference or one attribute difference between adversaries, and 12 of 27 cases with no hetero-geneity (44.4 percent) occurred in the Western Hemisphere. Europe, at the other end of the spectrum, had no such cases. A modest proportion of the cases for Africa, the Middle East, and Asia had total homogeneity, 14.1 percent, 7.3 percent, and 2.9 percent, respectively. Crises with two attribute differences between adversaries were concentrated in Europe, followed by Asia and Africa. Those with three attribute differences occurred most frequently in Europe, the Middle East, and Africa. And maximal heterogeneity was especially evident in Asia, accounting for half or more of the crises in that region.

Interestingly, an expected association between the number of crisis actors and the extent of heterogeneity in crises is not supported by the data: 89.9 percent of the Asian cases and 87.7 percent of Europe's crises were characterized by two or more attribute differences, but only 17.4 percent of the former and 38.6 percent of the latter were multiple-actor (three or more) cases.

Issues

The breakdown of crisis issues by system and geography is contained in Tables 15 and 16. As evident in Table 15, the military-security (M-S) issue-area is preeminent for the 50-year period as a whole, accounting for 47.8 percent of the 278 international crises; and when cases focusing on an M-S issue and one other issue-area are added, the proportion of the total set rises to 79.1 percent. At the other end of the spectrum only 16.6 percent of all crises did not relate to the M-S issue-area, three-fourths of these affecting only one issue-area.

Comparing across systems, there was not much substantive difference in the distribution among all categories of issues for the three pre– and post–World War II systems, though it is noteworthy that the bipolar system accounted for 7 of the 12 triple issue-area crises.

In terms of regional distribution (Table 16), there were few significant variations from the overall proportion of cases in the M-S issue-area alone. The same applies to the combined M-S plus M-S and one other issue-area categories. Among three-issue cases, Europe had about twice the overall average of 4.3 percent. In the non-M-S categories combined, Europe had somewhat more than the average— 24.6 percent compared to 16.6 percent—and Asia noticeably fewer, with 10.1 percent.

Violence

The distribution of violence in crises, by system and geography, is presented in Tables 17 and 18. For the overall 50-year period, the cases were distributed almost equally among the four categories: no violence, minor clashes, serious clashes, and full-scale war. Viewed in terms of the nonviolence-violence dichotomy, however, violence was present in three-fourths of the 278 international crises, at a high level of intensity in half of the total set. Viewed in a different perspective, there was no violence at all in one-fourth of environmental changes in world politics in which decisionmakers perceived an increased probability of military hostilities.

Comparing across systems, violence increased as the number of members grew: The multipolar system of the 1930s was the least violent, with no violence in 39.5 percent of its crises, followed by the larger bipolar system (30.1 percent) and the much larger polycentric system (19 percent). There was no variation for minor clashes except, as expected, for crises during World War II. Serious clashes were proportionately more frequent after 1945 than before. Full-scale war was prevalent in 1939–1945 cases. More striking, a trend to greater violence is evident both from the 1930s to the post-1945 period as a whole and from multipolar to bipolar to polycentric international system: 13.2 percent to 24.7 percent to 31.9 percent in serious clashes, respectively, and, for high-intensity violence (serious clashes and war combined), 36.9 percent to 40.8 percent to 56.9 percent.

Comparing the systems across the violence categories gives the following results: crises in the multipolar system—a much higher proportion of no-violence cases than the average for that category, a lower proportion for serious clashes; bipolar cases—a lower proportion with full-scale war; polycentric cases—a higher proportion of serious clashes; and World War II cases, as expected, full-scale war preeminent.

As evident in Table 18, crises in Europe were the least violent, followed by those in the Americas. The most violent crisis region in terms of full-scale war was Asia. Using a broader criterion for "most violent," Asia accounted for 34.1 percent of all crises during the half century with serious clashes or full-scale wars. At the other extreme was the Americas (5.7 percent), where domestic violence is prevalent.

The largest concentration-of-violence categories for each region are as follows: for Asia, war; for Europe, no violence; for Americas, minor clashes and no violence; for Middle East, serious clashes; for Africa, serious clashes.

EMPIRICAL LINKAGES AMONG INDICATORS

Although the components of severity and importance have been combined to form indices, it would be incorrect to proceed without examining their empirical connections for two reasons. The first pertains to validity. Even though the structure of each index has been derived deductively, it is essential that the indicators show some empirical linkage to each other; each component is supposed to represent an aspect of the same general phenomenon. The second reason for correlating the indicators is to make sure that they are not too well-connected. An extreme amount of overlap would suggest that one or more of the components is superfluous.

On the basis of these two considerations, a moderate level of association among the constituents would be desirable. As can be deduced from the data in Tables 19 and 20, the components of severity and importance have that property. For each index, all constituents are positively correlated at better than the 5 percent level of significance. However, also as desired, the connections between them are not overwhelming: The coefficients (from Kendall's tau) range from 0.11 to 0.53, suggesting that no indicator of either severity or importance merely duplicates another.

OVERALL SEVERITY

As expected, the most severe crises group was that including cases from 1939 to 1945 (Table 21). If the World War II period is omitted, average overall severity declined over time and system: multipolar (1929–1939), 4.17; bipolar (1945–1962), 3.96; polycentric (1963–1979), 3.60. This decline suggests a long-term twentieth-century trend toward greater stability (diminishing instability) of, and more effective coping with crisis by, the global system as a whole. The trend, or tendency, is also consistent with the earlier findings about superpower and great power involvement in crises. The powers currently managing the system appear to be acting more cautiously than their predecessors, and this caution is reflected in lower severity scores.

Stated in more general terms, the average severity figures appear to be inconsistent with the conventional wisdom about systemic evolution. For example, world models such as those described in *World Dynamics* (Forrester, 1973) and *The Limits to Growth* (Meadows et al., 1972) have suggested that the system is headed toward self-destruction. If these (and other) models are correct, systemic crises logically should become more severe over time rather than less. That has not been the case. Although it may be argued that these studies have focused on a different level of analysis and on somewhat different issues (economic development versus military security), the absence of a trend toward higher severity still seems counter to their pessimistic viewpoints.

In terms of geography, Europe and Asia stand out as the regions with the highest average severity scores, 4.73 and 4.35, respectively, with the Middle East a not-too-distant third (3.98). Even if one excludes the World War II cases with their high severity scores, Europe and Asia maintain their dominant positions.

MOST SEVERE INTERNATIONAL CRISES

The most severe (MS) international crises from 1929 to 1979 are the 26 cases with the highest overall severity out of the 278-case population, or approximately 10 percent of the data set. Their overall scores range from 10.00 to 6.77 on our 10-point scale. The distribution of these cases in time and space, along with their individual severity and importance scores, is presented in Table 22.

Europe was the preeminent region of severe international crises for the half century under inquiry, accounting for 12 of the 26 most severe cases and a much higher proportion of the total Europe-located crises than the MS proportion of total cases in any other region: Europe, 12 of 57 cases (21.1 percent); Middle East, 5 of 55 cases (9.1 percent); Asia, 5 of 69 cases (7.2 percent); Africa, 3 of 64 cases (4.7 percent); and the Americas, 1 of 33 cases (3.1 percent). As expected, all 5 MS crises in the 1930s and 3 of the 4 during World War II took place in Europe. Thereafter, the geographical distribution of very high-severity crises became diffuse. During the bipolar period (1945–1962), four regions were represented: 4 crises in Asia, 3 each in Europe and the Middle East, and 1 in the Americas. And in the polycentric period (1963–1979), the MS crises were concentrated in the Third World: 3 in Africa and 2 in the Middle East, with 1 in Europe. In short, the end of European colonial empires and the trebling of the number of state actors in the global system were accompanied inter alia by the spread of very high-severity crises beyond the European core to the former geo-political-economic periphery of Asia, Africa, and the Middle East.

Viewed in terms of time, the most severe crises declined in frequency from the bipolar to the polycentric period, 11 to 6, during an identical time span, 17 years in each period. The greatest concentration of MS cases was the three-year period 1956–1959 with 4 crises, Suez, Berlin Deadline, Taiwan Straits II, and Lebanon-Iraq Upheaval. In the time domain as well, the proportional distribution of very high-severity crises was stable for the first three periods: 1929–1939 (5 of 38 cases, that is, 1 for 7.6 cases), 1939–1945 (4 of 31, that is, 1 for 7.75 cases), 1945–1962 (11 of 93 cases, that is, 1 for 8.5 cases). In the polycentric period, 1963–1979, there was a sharp decrease (6 for 116, that is, 1 for every 19 cases). In general, this indicates declining intensity of international crises from the onset of polycentrism.

As evident in Table 23, the MS crises from 1929 to 1979 that occurred in the Middle East had the highest average intensity (8.65). Moreover, there were two broad regional groupings, in terms of average overall severity of crises: Africa and the Middle East (8.20–8.65); and the Americas, Europe, and Asia (7.58–7.98). In the time domain, the average score for MS crises was almost identical in 1929–1939 and 1939–1945, that is, in a period of relative peace and one of global war. The largest concentration of these crises occurred in the bipolar period, but their average intensity was the lowest of the four periods. The highest average intensity was in the polycentric period.

Many of the most severe crises were linked; they were recurring disturbances in the international system arising from a shared, unresolved issue. Two clusters were located in Europe, one in the 1930s over Germany's challenge to the post–World War I status quo, the other in the bipolar period over Berlin. One cluster focused on the Arab-Israel Conflict. A fourth cluster centered on the Korean War. And in Africa, two cases concerned Angola. Altogether, these clusters accounted for 14 of the 26 MS crises. Viewed in terms of protracted conflicts, 5 cases can be identified with the East-West conflict since 1945 (Azerbaijan, Berlin Blockade, Berlin Deadline, Berlin Wall, Cuban Missiles), 3 cases with the Arab-Israel conflict since 1948 (Suez, Six Day War, and October–Yom Kippur War), 3 cases within the Korea Conflict since 1950, and 2 cases within the Angola conflict since 1975.

The distribution of most severe crises in terms of power discrepancy between the adversaries and the resort to war is especially instructive. Of the 22 cases (the 4 intrawar crises during World War II are excluded because of lack of data), 18 were characterized by high power discrepancy (e.g., Prague Spring 1968, between the USSR and its Warsaw Pact allies on the one hand and Czechoslovakia on the other). However, full-scale war was present in only 7 of these 18 cases (e.g., Korean War I), whereas there was no violence in 6 of them (e.g., Remilitarization of the Rhineland). Conversely, 3 of the 4 cases characterized by low power discrepancy were accompanied by full-scale war (e.g., Korean War II, when the participation of the USSR drastically reduced the power discrepancy between the adversarial coalitions). These findings suggest that when states know or believe they will win a war, they do not have to fight, and that when states know or believe they will lose a war, they do not try. Stated differently, when crises are severe, states are more inclined to fight in a situation of uncertainty about the power balance, indicating a possibility of winning a war.

Severity Indicators

We turn now to a brief discussion of the data on the six severity indicators, that is, the components of overall severity, of the most severe international crises from 1929–1979 as a group. The individual scores are presented in Table 24.

The minimal number of crisis actors was 3, occurring in 2 cases (Cuban Missiles, with the United States, USSR, and Cuba, and Taiwan Straits II, with the PRC, Taiwan, and the United States). There were

4 crisis actors in 9 cases, 5 crisis actors in 6 cases, and 6 crisis actors in 5 cases. In 4 cases there were more than 6 crisis actors (Rhineland, 7; Angola, 7; Pearl Harbor, 10; Entry into World War II, 21). For the entire set of 278 international crises, there was 1 crisis actor in 107 cases and 2 crisis actors in 107 cases, comprising 77 percent of all cases. Thus the participation of more than 2 crisis actors makes highly likely—but not necessary—very high severity for that crisis.

Until the end of World War II, the crisis actors in all most severe cases except 2 (Entry into World War II and Pearl Harbor) were located in the region where the crisis occurred (e.g., all 7 actors in the Remilitarization of the Rhineland were European states). A change in this respect began with the Azerbaijan Crisis in which three regions were represented: the Middle East (Iran), Europe (USSR), and the Americas (the United States). Multiregional participation in crises continued throughout the bipolar period (4 of 11 crises with actors from three regions, the rest from two regions) and the polycentric period (5 of 6 crises triregional in participants). In short, severe crises became more multiregional over time.

As for geostrategic salience, all but 1 of the 26 most severe crises had relevance beyond a single international system. Eleven cases were salient to the dominant system (of the great powers in the 1930s and of the superpowers since 1945), as well as to one subsystem. For example, in the Azerbaijan Crisis, the Middle East Subsystem was involved and the concerns were oil and the USSR's access to warm water ports; in the Prague Spring Crisis, the subsystem of Eastern European countries was involved and the concerns were the stability of Soviet hegemony and the East-West European balance. Six of the MS crises were salient to the dominant system and more than one subsystem (e.g., Rhineland and all three Berlin crises involved the balance of power between the great powers and the superpowers, respectively, and influence over Western and Eastern Europe).

Seven of these international crises had global geostrategic salience:

1. Entry into World War II, because of the worldwide location of its 21 crisis actors and the issues of ideological conflict and global hegemony.
2. Pearl Harbor, because of the physical globalization of World War II and the struggle for world mastery between the Axis and Allied Powers.
3. Korean War III, because of the implication of the possible use of nuclear weapons by the United States for all members of the global system.

4. Suez, because of the far-reaching significance of the participation of both superpowers and two great powers, France and the United Kingdom, and the salience of the Suez Canal to world trade, as well as access to Middle East oil.
5. Cuban Missiles, because of the near-nuclear confrontation between the United States and USSR, and its potential consequences for states and peoples everywhere.
6. Six Day War and October–Yom Kippur War, because of the intense, adversarial involvement of the superpowers in support of their clients and, in the latter, the oil embargo and the second near-nuclear confrontation between the United States and the USSR.

The Shaba case was an exception among MS cases because it did not have the expected high score in geostrategic salience. However, it scored sufficiently high in all other elements of severity to give it a high score for overall severity. Noteworthy, too, is the evidence that superpower participation in crises as crisis actors does not per se ensure global salience (e.g., in the three Berlin cases and the Azerbaijan Crisis).

A large majority of the most severe crises, 20 of 26, were characterized by maximal heterogeneity; that is, the pair of adversarial actors in a crisis with the widest gap differed on all four attributes—level of military capability, extent of economic development, type of political regime, and culture. In 3 cases, there were three attribute differences (in Fall of Western Europe—military, political, and cultural differences between Germany and Belgium; in Berlin Blockade and Berlin Deadline—military, political, and cultural differences between Britain or France and the USSR). There were 2 MS cases with two attribute differences (Munich and Invasion of Scandinavia), and 1 case with a single attribute difference (military capability between Czechoslovakia and the USSR in the Prague Spring Crisis). All three crises that failed to fulfill the expectation of a high score for heterogeneity (those with one or two attribute differences) took place in Europe. Noteworthy, too, is the strong correlation between maximal heterogeneity and high overall severity among the MS group of cases, 20/26, which is stronger than that between a high score for actors or geostrategic salience and a high overall score, 8/26 and 12/26, respectively.

Involvement by the great powers was intense, as expected, in a large majority of most severe crises, 20 of 26 scoring 5 or 6 on the involvement scales. Both superpowers were crisis actors in 11 of these cases (e.g., Korean War II, the three Berlin crises, Suez, Six Day War,

October–Yom Kippur War, Cuban Missiles), and in 5 other cases, during the 1930s and World War II, more than two great powers were crisis actors (e.g., Munich, Entry into World War II). In another 4 MS cases, one superpower was a crisis actor, the other highly involved (e.g., Korean War I, Taiwan Straits II). There were 4 high-severity crises with both the United States and USSR highly involved, through direct or indirect military aid, or with its 1930s counterpart, namely, one or two great powers as crisis actors (e.g., Rhineland crisis). And in 2 cases, one superpower was a crisis actor and the other was not involved or only marginally so (Korean War III, in which the United States was a direct participant, the USSR politically involved; Prague Spring, in which the USSR was a crisis actor, the United States was not involved at all). Thus, of the 6 exceptions to our expectation of a very high score for involvement by the superpowers or great powers, 4 cases occurred in the 1930s or World War II (Invasion of Albania, Invasion of Scandinavia, Fall of Western Europe, Rhineland) whereas 2 cases occurred after World War II (Korean War III and Prague Spring).

It is noteworthy that, of the 4 post–World War II MS crises with one superpower as crisis actor and the other highly involved, the pattern was constant, with the United States performing the former function, the USSR the latter: The Soviet Union sent military aid to the United States' adversary but avoided a direct confrontation. Moreover, of the 11 cases in which both superpowers were crisis actors, 7 occurred during the bipolar period and 4 in the polycentric period; that is, the change in polarity was accompanied by less direct confrontation between the superpowers. Two issues dominated U.S.-USSR confrontation: Berlin and the Arab-Israel Conflict. At the same time, both superpowers were adversarial crisis actors in all five regions.

Only 1 of the 26 most severe crises—Lebanon-Iraq Upheaval—did not focus on a military-security issue. Seventeen MS cases were over military-security and another type of issue (Pearl Harbor, military/economic; Suez, military/political; Angola, military/political). Six cases of very high severity focused on the military-security issue-area alone (e.g., Entry into World War II, Cuban Missiles). And 2 crises were multiple issue in character (Berlin Wall, military/political/status; Prague Spring, military/political/status).

More than half of the most severe crises, 14 of 26, involved the highest level of violence, namely, full-scale war: In 10 of these cases, war preceded—and led to—crisis (e.g., Spanish Civil War, Suez); in the other 4 cases, crisis antedated and culminated in war (Invasion of Albania, Entry into World War II, Pearl Harbor, Six Day War). It is noteworthy that 3 of the crisis-leading-to-war cases rank among the highest in overall severity for the entire data set of 278 cases, including the cases with the first and second highest degrees of severity, Entry into World War II and Pearl Harbor. There were 4 high-severity cases involving serious clashes (e.g., Taiwan Straits II, Congo II) and 2 cases with minor clashes (e.g., Prague Spring). The 6 exceptions to an expectation of a high level of violence include several of the celebrated crises in the twentieth century (Rhineland, Munich, Azerbaijan, the three Berlin crises). Notwithstanding the absence of violence, they all scored high in overall severity because of high scores in most of their other components. In short, a high level of violence alone, like a high score for any of the six components, is not a necessary condition of inclusion in the select group of most severe international crises.

Key Crisis Dimensions

The 26 most severe international crises from 1929 to 1979 will now be examined in terms of their frequency distribution along key crisis dimensions: trigger or breakpoint; value threat; crisis management technique; centrality of violence; severity of violence; duration; activity of global organization; effectiveness of global organization activity; content of outcome; and form of outcome.

Trigger (Breakpoint). Among the 26 most severe crises during the half century under inquiry, half were catalyzed by violent acts: Eight were from external sources (e.g., the attack on South Korea by North Korean forces on 25 June 1950, the Korean War I case, and the attack by Soviet-backed Movimento Popular de Liberacao de Angola (MPLA) forces against the Frente Nacional de Libertacao de Angola (FNLA) headquarters in Luanda on 12 July 1975, triggering the Angola Crisis); the other 5 were internal physical challenges to the regime of a state (e.g., the revolt against the Spanish Republic by the Franco-led Falange army coalition on 17 July 1936). Six international crises of very high severity were set in motion by nonviolent military acts (e.g., the emplacement of Soviet offensive missiles in Cuba in 1962, triggering the Missiles Crisis). Six crises were initiated by political acts (e.g., the publication by the three Western Powers in June 1948 of their March London Conference recommendation to integrate the U.S., British, and French zones in Germany, triggering the Berlin Blockade Crisis). And 1 crisis, Berlin Wall 1961, was catalyzed by an external change.

Value Threat. The highest value that actors in each of the 26 most severe international crises perceived to be threatened was one of three: Existence was at stake in 11 cases (e.g., for Czechoslovakia in the Munich Crisis and for Israel in the Six Day War Crisis); grave damage was anticipated in 8 cases (e.g., by both the PRC and Taiwan in the Taiwan Straits Crisis, 1958, and by Egypt and Israel in the October–Yom Kippur War); and influence was the highest value threatened in 7 cases (e.g., by the United States and Britain in the Azerbaijan Crisis, and by the Soviet Union in the Prague Spring Crisis).

Crisis Management Technique. Violence was the pervasive crisis management technique (CMT) in the most severe international crises from 1929 to 1979: It was the primary CMT in 12 of the 26 cases and was present in 7 others (e.g., the first two Korean War crises and, for violence as a coequal CMT with one or more others, the Suez-Sinai War). There were 3 cases in which nonviolent military acts were the primary CMT (e.g., Cuban Missiles); another 3 with negotiation or a combination of pacific CMTs (e.g., the Remilitarization of the Rhineland Crisis); and 1 case with nonmilitary pressure as the primary CMT (Azerbaijan).

Centrality of Violence. As for the centrality of violence in crisis management, it was preeminent in 11 of the 26 most severe cases (e.g., Pearl Harbor, Six Day War, and Shaba). It was important but supported by other CMTs in 8 other cases of high overall severity (e.g., Invasion of Albania Crisis, Korean War III, and Lebanon-Iraq Upheaval). In none of these cases did violence play a minor role. It was absent as a crisis management technique in 7 cases (e.g., Cuban Missiles and the three Berlin crises).

Severity of Violence. Violence was very intense as a crisis management technique in the most severe international crises. Actors resorted to full-scale war in half of the 26 cases (e.g., the Spanish Civil War, several World War II cases like the Fall of Western Europe, Korean War I and II, Six Day War, October–Yom Kippur War). There were serious clashes in 5 cases (e.g., Lebanon-Iraq Upheaval) and minor clashes only in the Prague Spring Crisis. The remaining 7 cases, as noted, were without violence as a CMT.

Duration. A large majority of the most severe crises, 19 of 26, were of long duration, that is, 61 days or more (e.g., Spanish Civil War, almost three years, Berlin Blockade, almost a year, Prague Spring, six months). There were 5 medium-duration cases, 32–60 days (Rhineland, Munich, Entry into World War II, Fall of Western Europe, Cuban Missiles). And 2 of these cases lasted less than 32 days (Invasion of Albania, Six Day War).

Global Organization: Highest Activity. There was no involvement by the global organization in 9 of the 26 most severe crises (e.g., Munich, Berlin Wall, Shaba II). In 3 cases, the League of Nations or the United Nations engaged in discussion but did not pass a resolution (e.g., Taiwan Straits II). The global organization did pass an operative resolution in 8 crises: 3 UN calls for a cease-fire (e.g., Six Day War Crisis); 2 condemnations (Rhineland, Angola); and 3 calls for action by member-states (e.g., by the USSR and Iran in the Azerbaijan Crisis). There were 2 cases of mediation (Berlin Blockade, Cuban Missiles). Emergency military forces were dispatched in 2 others (Korean War I, Suez). An observer group was sent in 1 case (Lebanon-Iraq Upheaval). And there was 1 case of general UN activity (attempted conciliation by the secretary-general in the Berlin Deadline Crisis).

Global Organization: Effectiveness. Global organization activity in the most severe international crises from 1929 to 1979 was ineffective on the whole. There was no League of Nations/UN involvement in 9 of 26 cases. In 10 others, their activity did not contribute to crisis abatement (e.g., Rhineland, Berlin Blockade). It had an important, positive effect in 3 of these crises (in Azerbaijan, the Security Council applied pressure on the USSR to reach an amicable withdrawal agreement with Iran; in Suez Crisis, the UN passed cease-fire resolutions and dispatched a UN Emergency Force (UNEF) to Sinai; in Cuba Crisis, mediation was undertaken by the secretary-general and the UN supervised the withdrawal of Soviet missiles from the island). However, in 3 other cases, activity by the global organization escalated the crisis (in Korean War II, the crossing of the 38th parallel by UN forces brought China into the war; in Lebanon-Iraq Upheaval, the dispatch of an inadequate observer group that was ineffective in curbing infiltration into Lebanon prolonged that crisis; in Six Day War, the withdrawal of UNEF from Sinai escalated the crisis by removing a 10-year barrier to direct military confrontation between Egypt and Israel). Finally, in 1 case (October–Yom Kippur War), the UN contributed marginally to crisis deescalation.

Outcome: Content. A large majority of the most severe international crises, 19 of 26, terminated with an ambiguous outcome from the crisis actors' perspectives; that is, they resulted in some combination of defeat, victory, stalemate, or compromise between the adversaries, other than a strict defeat-victory pairing. The other 7 cases ended with a definitive result, that is, with a defeat-victory outcome. Among them were several celebrated crises of the 50-year period: the Berlin Blockade, with defeat for the USSR and victory for the three Western Powers; the Cuban Missile Crisis, with a (thinly concealed) defeat for the Soviet Union and Cuba and a (self-constrained) victory for the United States; and the Six Day War, with a (dramatic) defeat for Egypt, Jordan, and Syria and a victory for Israel.

Outcome: Form. Almost two-thirds of the most severe international crises, 15 of 26, ended with a formal or semiformal agreement between the adversaries (e.g., the Munich Agreement among France, Germany, Italy, and the United Kingdom; a Soviet-Iran withdrawal of forces agreement, based upon a UN Security Council Resolution, in the Azerbaijan Crisis; semiformal agreements between the Soviet Uinon and the Western Powers or the United States, ending the Berlin Blockade Crisis and the Cuban Missile Crisis). There was a tacit agreement in 1 case (Taiwan Straits II). The other 10 cases ended without agreement, 7 of them through a unilateral act by the victorious adversary(ies) (e.g., Germany's rejection of any constraint on its remilitarization of the Rhineland, military triumph by the Franco-Germany-Italy coalition in the Spanish Civil War, the USSR's un-qualified support for the permanence of the Berlin Wall).

The data on the 26 most severe international crises from 1929 to 1979 indicate the configuration for this subset (Table 25).

Importance Level of Crises

Certain patterns have emerged from the descriptive analysis of the most severe (MS) crises in the data set. Spatial and temporal regularities are but two such examples. As a logical extension, the importance levels of these cases will be investigated. This inquiry will be pursued in three stages. The first two will consist of the identification of regional and temporal patterns. The third stage will concern specific categories of importance (i.e., changes in power, actors, rules, and alliances) and the impact of MS crises upon them.

Regional and Temporal Patterns. As noted, crises in the MS subset have tended to occur in Europe (12 of 26). Cases in that region have exhibited a wide range of importance scores. At one extreme is the World War II cluster (1939–1945), with the highest possible score (10.00); at the other is Berlin Deadline (1957–1959) with a value of 1.75. (The cases in between generally have scored rather high on both scales.) Of the two specific cases mentioned, explanation of the latter crisis certainly is more troubling than that for the former. How could such a severe crisis prove to be of so little importance to the international system? An explanation for the discrepancy may be formulated with reference to other MS cases in the European cell for 1945–1962 (Table 22). All three cases included in that category pertain to Berlin, with the Blockade case (1948-1949) being by far the most important. Perhaps the airlift confrontation established a regime for future Soviet-American interactions over similar issues, thus dampen-ing the potential long-term effects of subsequent crises. In other words, a series of cases may reflect certain precedents set in the first iteration.[37]

Although Europe has been the most frequent location of cases in the MS subset, there does not appear to be a regional bias with regard to importance scores. Among the five Middle East cases, the scores are ranged from 3.63 to 7.38, and for Africa, from 2.13 to 5.50. Although the Americas are represented by only one crisis, the Cuban Missiles case (1962) ranks high in importance. In sum, MS cases have tended to be European based but not to the exclusion of other locations for important crises.

As evident in Table 26, temporal variations in importance are pronounced, even apart from the intra-war period, 1939–1945: an average of 6.91 for 1929–1939 and much lower after World War II, 4.67 for 1945–1962 and 5.25 for 1963–1979.

Changes Resulting from MS Crises. It may be instructive to probe the importance of the MS crises in more specific terms. As noted, there are four categories of change that combine to represent the importance of a crisis: (1) actors, (2) alliances, (3) power, and (4) rules of the game. Perhaps the MS crises will tend to produce change in some categories more than in others. This in fact appears to be the case.

With respect to power, the modal outcome is change in the relative status of adversarial actors, although the margin is not overwhelming. Only in the cases of Entry into World War II (1939–1945) and Korean War (1950–1953) did the maximal change occur. In the former, Germany and Japan exited from the apex of power; in the latter, the PRC moved into the inner circle.

Changes in actors are uncommon even for the MS subset. About one-half of the crises have produced no change in regime or even orientation among participants. At the other end of the continuum, only one case, Entry into World War II, resulted in the elimination or creation of state actors.

Rules of the game have been much more susceptible to change. Only the Invasion of Albania (1939) and Shaba II (1978) have been without effects upon informal or institutionalized rules. This component of the Importance Index clearly distinguishes the MS subset from crises in general, because most cases do not produce significant rule changes.

With respect to alliances, the cases are distributed evenly across the four possible categories of change. This represents more change than would be expected from the data set in general. Several cases (Rhineland, 1936; Entry into World War II, 1939; Korean War III,

1953; and the Yom Kippur War, 1973-1974) actually resulted in the elimination or formation of alliances.

Anomalies. During the course of this investigation of the Index of Importance for MS crises, some interesting anomalies have emerged. One is that cases for Africa have been relatively low in importance. Another is the vast difference between severity (8.25) and importance (1.75) for the Berlin Deadline, easily the largest discrepancy in the data set. Both of these unexpected developments will be assessed in terms of specific indicators of importance, in the hope that a component analysis will prove enlightening.

For the cases of Congo II (1964), Angola (1975-1976), and Shaba II (1978) there is a common result concerning the distribution of power: None of these cases produced more than a change in the relative power of crisis actors. Crises in Africa have had a low priority for states at the top of the power hierarchy, and this has truncated the range of importance scores because even severe cases will not result in change at the apex of power. Importance of African crises thus will be less sensitive to increasing severity than crises in other regions.

The Berlin Deadline case is striking in that it produced no changes in actors, alliances, or power. Although it did result in a breakdown of the consensus on Berlin, the crisis did not have the impact expected from its high severity score. As noted, the Berlin Deadline Crisis took place long after some important characteristics of the dominant subsystem had been established. Alliances were firmly in place on the issue of Berlin. Power changes were inhibited by the crucial nature of the city because a complete victory for one side or the other almost certainly could not occur short of a nuclear exchange. The same is true for changes in actors. In sum, the crisis challenged the existing equilibrium (so it was rated a crisis of high severity or instability), but the original equilibrium remained intact (so the impact of the crisis made it one of low importance or disequilibrium).

Severity and Importance:
Two Case Studies

The method used to derive the severity and importance scores for the international crises in the data set, 1929–1979, can be demonstrated with the assigned scores for the 1973-1974 Middle East Crisis and the Angola Crisis of 1975-1976, in Tables 27 and 28. For ease of exposition the scores for overall severity and overall importance have been converted to 10-point scales, with 1.00 as the minimum and 10.00 as the maximum.[38]

MIDDLE EAST CRISIS, 1973-1974

The October–Yom Kippur Crisis of 1973-1974 is one of the three most severe and most important cases in the Middle East data subset (the others are the Suez-Sinai Campaign of 1956-1957 and the Six Day War of 1967).[39] The crisis of 1973-1974 began on 5 October with evidence of an impending massive disruption in the high level of conflictual interaction between Israel and its Arab adversaries. A concerted military attack by Egypt and Syria the next day and other events that followed posed a serious challenge to the structure of the Middle East subsystem and, toward the end of the crisis, a challenge to the dominant system as well. The result, as reached from the 10 indicators listed in Table 12, is very high scores for overall severity (9.18) and overall importance (6.63).

Background

The West Bank of the Jordan River, the Gaza Strip, the Sinai Peninsula, and the Golan Heights had been occupied by Israel since the Six Day War of June 1967. In March 1969, Egypt launched a war of attrition against Israeli forces in the Sinai. A U.S.-sponsored cease-fire was accepted by both sides in August 1970—but not a U.S. plan for peace in the region, the Rogers Proposals. In April 1973, Israel's forces were mobilized when its leaders perceived Egyptian exercises to be a prelude to an invasion of Israel; the invasion was to occur six months later.

On 13 September 1973, 13 Syrian MIGs and one Israeli Mirage were shot down in an air battle over the Golan Heights. When Syria did not react immediately to this dramatic defeat, some Israeli leaders became suspicious that Damascus was planning a major retaliation. The Israel Defense Forces (IDF) in the north were strengthened, and precautionary measures were taken in the south. Syria's massing of three infantry divisions, tanks, and artillery and a mobilization of Syrian reserves, along with the evacuation of Soviet military advisers and their families from Damascus and Cairo, were all noted by Israeli intelligence. The IDF was put on the highest state of alert. Nevertheless, as late as 3 October 1973, Israel's military intelligence perceived an outbreak of war in the immediate future to be very unlikely. This erroneous judgment was based on two Israeli misperceptions: that Egypt's inferior air power would not permit it to launch a war against

Israel and that Syria would not "go it alone" without Egypt's active participation.

Severity

Actors. Five states became crisis actors at different times during the Middle East Crisis of 1973-1974: Israel (5 October), Syria (10 October), the United States (12 October), Egypt (18 October), and the Soviet Union (22 October). The many involved actors included Arab states from the Near East Core such as Iraq and Saudi Arabia and from North Africa, like Algeria, Libya, and Morocco. These states supported the Arab crisis actors by several means, including the dispatch of token military contingents to the battlefield and a draconian oil price increase, along with an oil embargo against the Netherlands and the United States.

A deployment of Egyptian forces toward the Suez Canal on 5 October 1973 and a change from a defensive to an offensive posture triggered a crisis for Israel. At the same time, Israel's military intelligence reported an impending Egyptian attack across the canal scheduled for the following day. Israel immediately raised the IDF alert level and strengthened its forces along the northern and southern borders. The war began on 6 October with a simultaneous attack by Egyptian and Syrian forces. By 10 October, after heavy losses, Israeli forces succeeded in reversing the tide of battle in the north, triggering a crisis for Syria. Syria responded not only on the battlefield but also with an urgent call for an increase of Egyptian military pressure on Israel in the south and an appeal to the Soviet Union for aid. During the next three days, Israeli forces advanced 10 kilometers beyond the 1967 cease-fire lines into Syrian territory.

Israeli Prime Minister Golda Meir agreed to a cease-fire in place on 12 October. Its rejection by Egypt and Syria triggered a crisis for the United States, which feared a possible confrontation with the USSR: Seven Soviet airborne divisions had been placed on an increased state of readiness. The Soviet commitment to the Arabs, in the form of a massive resupply of arms by air and sea, indicated to Washington that Moscow would not tolerate an unambiguous Arab defeat, comparable to that in 1967.

The successful Egyptian crossing of the Suez Canal was followed on 14 October by the largest tank battle in military history, with Egypt suffering a major defeat. On 16 October, the Israelis crossed the canal and threatened to surround the Egyptian Third Army. A crisis for Egypt was triggered with President Anwar Sadat became aware of the country's worsening military position. Egypt's response was to press the Soviet Union to obtain a cease-fire agreement. This accord was hastily arranged by Leonid Brezhnev and Henry Kissinger in Moscow on 19–20 October, and the first cease-fire of the 1973 war, formally imposed by the UN, took effect on 22 October. When the Egyptians continued their attempt to open up an escape route for their Third Army, fighting broke out once more.

Israeli violations of the 22 October cease-fire agreement triggered a crisis for the Soviet Union. Moscow responded on 24 October by dispatching naval vessels and sending a note from Brezhnev to Nixon containing a clear warning that, unless the Israeli onslaught on the west bank of the Suez Canal was stopped at once, the USSR might intervene unilaterally on the battlefield. The United States responded with mounting pressure on Israel to stop fighting and to allow nonmilitary supplies to reach the Third Army. At the same time, President Richard Nixon issued a sharp reply to Moscow; most of the U.S. armed forces, including the Strategic Air Command with its nuclear capability, were put on a high state of alert, namely "Defensive Condition 3." The crisis escalated further when, on 25 October, a Soviet freighter arrived in Alexandria reportedly carrying nuclear weapons. Finally, on 26 October 1973, a U.S.-Soviet-sponsored UN Security Council Resolution calling for a second cease-fire was accepted by all parties. Thus, in terms of the actor component, the October–Yom Kippur Crisis was one of the most severe international crises since the end of World War II, scoring 5 on a six-point scale of actor participation.

Involvement. The crisis of 1973-1974 was even more severe in terms of involvement by the superpowers (SPs), point 6 on a six-point scale. The United States and USSR were crisis actors in confrontation with each other, as demonstrated by the Soviet threat of direct military intervention in Sinai and the U.S. counterthreat, as expressed in the nuclear alert. Only the Cuban Missile Crisis of 1962 was more acute in the nuclear dimension of SP behavior.

More tangibly, both superpowers were lavish in supplying arms and equipment to their client states during and after the October–Yom Kippur War. The Soviets began a combined airlift-sealift on 8 October, the United States on 14 October. Apart from urgently needed replacements for Israeli planes and tanks lost on both fronts, the United States extended US$2.2 billion in emergency military assistance by the end of the war. Moreover, the cease-fire agreements were worked out between the SPs. Premier Aleksey Kosygin arrived in Cairo on 16 October to persuade Egypt to accept a cease-fire. Although Kosygin was at first unsuccessful, Soviet aerial reconnaissance persuaded Sadat within two days to accept this advice. Secretary of

State Kissinger visited Moscow on 19–20 October; he and Brezhnev hammered out a draft resolution for the UN Security Council, calling for an immediate cease-fire. The Security Council adopted this resolution within hours and authorized the creation of a UN force to police the Golan Heights.

The two superpowers remained dangerously involved during the peak stress phase of the 1973-1974 crisis, from 22 to 26 October. The Soviets, as noted, threatened to land paratroops to save the encircled Egyptian Third Army from destruction. The United States signaled its determination to prevent direct Soviet military intervention. Ultimately, Israel yielded to U.S. pressure on the Third Army issue, just as all the principal regional protagonists were to yield to U.S. mediation.

Talks between Egypt and Israel, with the active participation of Kissinger, continued for two months and concentrated on withdrawal to the post–Six Day War lines, the problem of the encircled Third Army, and the exchange of prisoners. A disengagement agreement was signed on 18 January 1974, with Israel agreeing to withdraw 20 kilometers from the Suez Canal, and with both parties agreeing to reduce the size of their forces. The negotiations between Israel and Syria took much longer, and U.S. involvement was no less intense or crucial for the outcome. Israel's demand for a complete list of all Israeli prisoners of war was negotiated by Kissinger in February 1974. In March, Syria announced that it had decided to resume the war immediately. Shelling of Israeli-held positions in the north and exchange of fire continued throughout spring 1974 in a miniwar of attrition. On 2 May, Kissinger began a month of shuttle diplomacy, traveling between Damascus and Jerusalem, with side trips to Riyadh, Amman, and Cairo. In the final U.S.-induced agreement, Israel returned parts of the Syrian town of Kuneitra but kept control over two of the three strategic hills in the area in which heavy weapons were forbidden. A UN buffer zone was established. As in the case of the Israel-Egypt Agreement, a U.S. Memorandum of Understanding, with pledges of large-scale military and economic aid, was given to Israel. The Israel-Syria Disengagement Agreement was signed on 31 May 1974, terminating the October–Yom Kippur Crisis for Israel, Syria, the Soviet Union, and the United States.

Geostrategic Salience. The geostrategic salience of the October–Yom Kippur Crisis was the maximum, that is, point 5 on a five-point scale. The Suez Canal is a key choke point in the transportation nexus between Europe, on one hand, and East Africa and South and Southeast Asia, on the other. Furthermore, the vast oil resources of the Gulf region and the rapid increase in petroleum prices, along with the embargo, made this crisis salient to the global system as a whole—to the dominant (superpower) system and almost all subsystems, which are dependent on a regular supply of imported oil.

The strategic significance of the Middle East is accentuated by two additional factors. Unlike Europe, this region remains a "grey zone" of competition in which the United States and USSR assume the right—and perceive the obligation—to be actively involved lest their adversary enhance its influence with one or more formally uncommitted states. Moreover, the location of the Middle East in close proximity to Soviet Central Asia, with its large Muslim population and centers of industrial-military development, gives this region very high power salience: to the United States, as a region of opportunity, along with economic and strategic resources; to the USSR, as a region of opportunity and high potential threat to the stability of heartland centers of population and industry. An international crisis in the Middle East and, especially within the Arab-Israel protracted conflict, is of higher salience to the superpowers than crises in any other Third World regional subsystem.

Heterogeneity. The October–Yom Kippur Crisis was among a substantial group of cases in the entire data set (93 of 278 or 33 percent) with the highest possible heterogeneity; that is, there were differences among pairs of adversaries on all four attributes—military capability, economic development, political regime, and cultural traits. Thus, although the principal regional protagonists (Egypt, Israel, and Syria) were small powers in global terms, each was confronted with a superpower allied to an adversary. Similarly, an economically underdeveloped Egypt faced the most advanced industrial state in the international system, the United States. There were several types of regimes, from Western democracy in one coalition (United States, Israel) to various kinds of authoritarianism in the other (the Communist USSR, the combined military-party regime in Syria, and the charismatic leader in Egypt. And in the cultural domain, Judaism faced Islam in the Israel-Arab confrontation. Heterogeneity in this crisis, notably cultural, was accentuated by acute dissensus on rules of the game among the Middle East crisis actors, for example, Arab nonrecognition of Israel's legitimacy and the corresponding Arab assumption of a right to expunge Israel as a sovereign state.

Issues. There were military and political issues in the 1973-1974 Middle East Crisis. Territory was a major focus of dispute, with Egypt and Syria trying to regain the territories they lost in the 1967 war, Sinai and the Golan Heights, respectively, and Israel striving to retain those territories as bargaining chips in future negotiations for a peace settlement. Borders, too, remained in dispute, within the larger territorial issue. For the superpowers, the principal issue was relative influence in a resource-rich, strategically located region of predominantly non-aligned states. And for the less powerful crisis actors, there were the additional issues of the regional military balance and the survival of Israel as a viable state. Thus, this indicator of the 1973-1974 crisis scored high but less than the maximum, 4 on a five-point scale.

Violence. The October–Yom Kippur Crisis ranks among the most severe of all post–World War II international crises in terms of violence. A full-scale war raged for 20 days. Casualties were in the tens of thousands. The tank battle of 14 October 1973 involved more than 2,000 tanks. Losses of equipment on both sides were staggering. This very costly conventional war was aggravated by a threat to use nuclear weapons, reportedly by Israel during the early days of setback on the battlefield, and potentially, though implicitly, by the United States through its nuclear alert. In short, the indicator of violence manifested the highest severity, 4 on a four-point scale, a full-scale war of exceptional intensity.

Taken together, the six indicators of severity in the October–Yom Kippur Crisis generate an overall score of 9.18, making it one of the five most severe cases in the ICB data set of 278 international crises from 1929 to 1979.

Importance

The 1973-1974 Middle East Crisis posed several challenges to the structure of the international system. At the global level, the oil embargo undermined the stability of the economies of Western Europe and Japan. In addition, many regions with underdeveloped economies came under grave pressure as a result of the unleashing of a powerful economic weapon on the part of the Arab states. Alliances were tested. The pre-1973 hierarchy of power in the Middle East was assaulted. And rule dissensus widened. What then were the consequences of this crisis for international systems in the years that followed?

Power Change. There were substantial changes in the distribution of power within the Arab-Israel subsystem. Israel had been the preeminent state in terms of regional capability following its overwhelming victory in the 1967 Six Day War. The 1973 war, however, marked the resurgence of Egypt's and Syria's military capability, along with a shift in the Middle East power hierarchy. Israel's brief tenure as regional superpower gave way to relative equality between Israel and Egypt at the apex of the Arab-Israel power pyramid, with Syria a serious contender for equal status. At a higher level of capability, it was a reversion to the hierarchy of power within the Arab-Israel system after the 1956-1957 Sinai-Suez Campaign.

As for the balance of influence between the superpowers in the Arab-Israel conflict zone, the United States seems to have been the principal beneficiary. Almost from the outset (8 October), it befriended Israel—but later Egypt as well. Through the cease-fire negotiations and beyond, the United States attained credibility as a mediator, in the world generally and among the crisis actors in particular. It seemed able to persuade them of empathy for Egyptian and Syrian goals, as well as for vital Israeli security interests. The U.S. role was enhanced by a change in its policy—namely, the supply of arms to Saudi Arabia and other lesser Arab states—at the same time that the historic commitment to Israel remained unchanged. The Soviets, by contrast, lost their effective bridgehead in Egypt; their support became confined to Syria. Thus the extent of power change registered 3 on a four-point scale—a shift in the power ranking of states within the system.

Actor Change. No actor was eliminated; nor were new ones created. However, regime orientations changed markedly. At the outset of the October–Yom Kippur Crisis, Egypt was a Soviet client, though less so than in the Gamal Nasser era. It remained almost entirely dependent upon the USSR for a wide range of advanced weapons, including bombers, fighter planes, and tanks, without which the military option to regain control of Sinai was not feasible. That dependence was even more glaring during the October–Yom Kippur War, when the Soviet combined sealift-airlift operation enabled Egypt to sustain the heavy losses in equipment from 6 October onward. Syria's dependence upon the Soviets was more striking at the outset and continued throughout the war, as replacements for lost equipment enabled the Syrian army to prevent an Israeli breakthrough to Damascus.

During the war, however, Egypt began the process of changing its alignment. Notwithstanding the Soviet threat to intervene on the battlefield in Egypt's favor, it was U.S. diplomatic pressure on Israel that rescued the Egyptian Third Army from annihilation. Moreover, it was Kissinger's mediation that led to the Egypt-Israel Disengagement Agreement of January 1974 and a partial Israeli withdrawal from the Suez Canal. A U.S. pledge to replace the Soviet Union as Egypt's principal arms supplier completed the process of a basic change in Egypt's orientation toward the superpowers at the conclusion of the crisis.

The shift in Egypt's alignment made the Soviets more interested in strengthening their Syria connection and made Syria more prepared to strengthen its alignment with Moscow. This regrouping had the major benefits for Syria of a steady and increasing flow of Soviet weapons, including advanced SAM batteries, planes, and tanks, along with Soviet diplomatic and political support. For Israel, the experience of 1973-1974 strengthened its dependence upon the United States— for arms, economic aid, and political and diplomatic support in international organizations, in which a pro-Arab phalanx in the Third World, supported by the Soviet bloc, threatened Israel's legitimacy as an international actor (e.g., the UN General Assembly's "Zionism as Racism" resolution of 1975). In short, actor change for this crisis registered 2 on a four-point scale.

Rules Change. Informal rules were maintained during the 1973 war, apart from a brief resort to surface-to-surface missiles by Syria, causing heavy damage and casualties to an Israeli kibbutz and a responsive bombing of urban centers by Israel. Much more significant was the setting in motion of a change in the basic rules of the Arab-Israel game, dramatized by Sadat's journey to Jerusalem in November 1977. The deeply rooted Arab consensus on Israel—politicide—was shattered by the ensuing Camp David Accords (1978) and the Egypt-Israel Peace Treaty (1979). Viewed in the perspective of this change in intra-Arab rules vis-à-vis Israel, the Hussein-Arafat accord of February 1985 is a continuation of the Arab search for a comprehensive peace settlement, including Palestinian self-determination, the raison d'être of their various forays into the arena of peace-making.

Alliance Change. Alliances were severely shaken by the 1973-1974 October–Yom Kippur Crisis. Fissures within NATO widened as the United States mounted an airlift to Israel whereas most of its European allies refused to cooperate. The cleavage widened further when the European Economic Community (EEC) issued a pro-Arab declaration of attitudes to the conflict on 6 November 1973, calling for Israeli withdrawal to the pre–5 June 1967 borders and affirming the Palestinian Arab unfettered right to self-determination. Within the Middle East, the alliance between Egypt and Syria crumbled under the weight of divergence of policy toward the superpowers, especially during the negotiations leading to the disengagement of forces. And the Sadat peace initiative in 1977, gestating during the aftermath of the 1973-1974 crisis, was to shatter the pattern of alliances among Middle East Arab states based upon, inter alia, the illegitimacy of Israel as a state. Taken together, this registered point 4 on the four-point scale for alliance change.

In short, the aftermath of the October–Yom Kippur Crisis was a transformation of the Middle East subsystem and basic change in the structure of both global and regional systems, which explains the very high score (6.63) for this crisis in terms of overall importance.

ANGOLA CRISIS, 1975-1976

The Angola Crisis was the most severe and one of the most important cases in Africa. It is interesting to speculate on why this war of national liberation in a remote region against a faltering colonial regime assumed such importance. As will become apparent from a review of scores for the 10 indicators, the internal concerns of the civil war were subsumed by external concerns imposed upon it.

Severity

Actors. Seven crisis actors ultimately emerged in the following sequence: the rival Angolan nationalist factions (that is, Angola itself), Zaire, Zambia, South Africa, Cuba, the Soviet Union, and the United States (scale point 6). In addition, there was an array of involved actors—China, Congo, North Korea, Portugal, Tanazania, and Yugoslavia, along with countries that made diplomatic efforts, Ivory Coast, Kenya, Nigeria, and Uganda, and nonstate actors such as the Organization of African Unity (OAU) and international financial interests.

Three nationalist groups, Movimento Popular de Libertacao de Angola (MPLA), Frente Nacional de Libertacao de Angola (FNLA), and Uniao Nacional Para a Independencia Total de Angola (UNITA), were created in opposition to Portuguese colonialism. They began jockeying for position against each other after the leftist coup in Portugal on 24 April 1974, with the new regime's decision to decolonize as quickly as possible. The Alvor Agreement of 15 January 1975 provided for independence to be granted on 10 November 1975 to a coalition government that would be representative of all three groups, as chosen through legislative elections in October. This agreement never succeeded in achieving peace and was annulled de facto in March 1975 when FNLA troops attacked MPLA forces north of the capital, Luanda. President Jomo Kenyatta of Kenya mediated a cease-fire on 21 June, but it was broken immediately. By July there existed a state of open warfare in Angola. The MPLA began receiving larger quantities of arms from the USSR, whereas the U.S.-backed FNLA concluded an alliance with UNITA and in August formally declared war on the MPLA.

Zambia became directly involved in the crisis on 12 July because of its concern about the consequences of a violent conflict being waged in a border state, especially when the essential Benguela railroad was closed down. A pro-Western stance initially led Zambia to support UNITA. This state also was influenced by the fact that

UNITA forces controlled the portion of Angola bordering its territory. Zambia's fragile economy was taxed further by the flood of Angolan refugees taking sanctuary in the state's western region. Being landlocked, they were dependent on Angolan territory and transport facilities for the export of copper and other goods. Zambia shifted policy and lent vocal, if not active, support to the MPLA once it realized that only the MPLA had the resources to keep the railway open and to stem the flow of refugees across the border.

Zaire's President Mobutu Seke Sekou initially supported the FNLA out of a sense of Bakongo nationalism. Moreover, Zaire's position as the "key to American foreign policy in sub-Saharan Africa" (Klinghoffer, 1980:92) appears to have been a factor in its perceiving a crisis in Angola, as did the United States. Mobutu allowed the United States to transfer arms to Angola through Zaire, and he sent Zairean commando units to fight with FNLA troops. However, once the MPLA was assured of victory, Mobutu announced that any Angolan refugees using Zaire as a base for operations against Angola would be expelled. Thus ended Zaire's participation in the crisis.

South Africa invaded Angola, through Namibia, on 23 October 1975, in support of FNLA and UNITA forces. Because of this action other Africans perceived these nationalist groups as collaborating with South Africa's white supremacist regime. Thus, greater legitimacy was accorded the MPLA and, by extension, their Soviet and Cuban sponsors (Marcum, 1978:273). By mid-November, MPLA and Cuban troops had stalled South Africa's advance. In January 1976, South Africa withdrew as a direct result of the U.S. Congress's ban on military aid to Angola because this ban demonstrated the United States' unwillingness to make a full-scale commitment to anti-Soviet forces in southern Africa.

South Africa clearly intervened out of concern for the regional balance of power. Already wary about the existence of an intractably hostile regime in Angola, the country was alarmed further by the MPLA's collaboration with the South-West African People's Organization (SWAPO), which had been waging a guerrilla campaign for independence in Namibia. Thus the Angola crisis provided South Africa with an opportunity to attack SWAPO. South Africans hoped to establish a friendly regime in Angola and to prompt some measure of gratitude from Zambia and Zaire. The South Africans were also anxious to show the United States that they stood as a strong and dedicated bullwark against communism in Africa.

Tanzania and Congo (Brazzaville) were involved regional actors. The latter, because of its relationship with the USSR, permitted the MPLA to establish headquarters in Brazzaville in 1963 and later allowed Cuban advisers to train MPLA troops in its territory. Tanzania initially supported the FNLA, permitting it to set up headquarters in Dar es Salaam. However, when South Africa intervened on its behalf, Tanzania shifted support to the MPLA, which was not tainted by contact with the apartheid regime.

China was the leading non-African power among the involved actors in the crisis. Beijing began sending aid to Angolan nationalists in 1971. The Chinese did this in an evenhanded manner through the OAU's Liberation Committee, which was then distributing funds to all three factions. In June 1974 they sent military instructors to Zaire to train FNLA fighters and in August began supplying them with light arms. According to John A. Marcum, China was motivated by a "consuming rivalry with the Soviet Union and eager[ness] to parley excellent relations in East Africa and Zaire into an Angolan shutout of the Russians" (1978:264). However, despite their continued support for the FNLA and UNITA, the Chinese withdrew from the crisis in July 1975, "in response to the OAU's call for neutrality among the three rival Angolan movements. The reason they gave for this decision was that since they were not in a position to deliver aid to the MPLA, they would have been taking sides if they were left supporting only the FNLA and UNITA. . . . Peking was not equipped to compete with massive Soviet aid" (Legum, 1977:156).

Involvement. Both the United States and the Soviet Union were active semimilitarily, and both were crisis actors (scale point 6). Since Cuba's actions during the crisis had an important connection to those of the USSR, it will be included in the analysis of superpower involvement.

U.S. policies toward Angola were essentially reactive to Soviet behavior and the MPLA initiatives. Washington was concerned with the amount of aid the USSR sent to the MPLA. Thus, the U.S. Central Intelligence Agency (CIA) covertly funneled US$31.7 million to the FNLA in August and September 1975 (Uttley, 1979:25). Marcum assessed U.S. policy as follows:

> American action and reaction seemed almost designed to provoke the Russians into seeking maximum advantage. Because the Soviet Union's outreach as a superpower is more military than economic, and because its capacity to intervene is essentially uncontrained by democratic accountability, there might have been every reason to conclude that the Soviets would enjoy an advantage in the event of an Angolan war by proxy. (1976:416)

Such a reactive policy rarely, if ever, leads to victory. In fact, the head of the CIA's Angola Task Force claimed his objective was not victory but was rather to "prevent an easy victory by communist-backed forces" (Stockwell, 1978:46). This objective was to be accomplished though the covert supply of arms and money to the FNLA and UNITA. The most disturbing facet of the United States' crisis management was that, in a complex case involving many internal and external actors, it responded only to the East-West dimension of the crisis.

Partially because their policy was reactive, U.S. leaders perceived a crisis in Angola. Their time to make decisions was limited by MPLA gains and by the fact that they were always reacting to Soviet policy decisions concerning the country. Influence in the region—a basic value—was threatened, as was the stability of states whose regimes they supported (e.g., Zaire, Zambia). Since the ultimate level of escalation to be attained during the crisis was unknown, U.S. military involvement became a distinct possibility, although Congressional constraints ultimately made that unfeasible.

Investigating superpower crisis management in a more general context, J. Wilkenfeld and Brecher (1982:194) found that nonviolent military action (e.g., mobilization, dispatch of troops) was the dominant Soviet crisis technique (45 percent), whereas the United States rarely utilized that method (13 percent). This would suggest that Washington was pursuing an ineffective strategy against the wrong adversary in Angola. Given that the Soviets seized the initiative (and because nonviolent military action is their dominant crisis management technique), they were more prepared to make a lasting and total commitment to their clients. Thus it would appear that the Soviets pursued a more rationally calculated crisis management.

The USSR had been sending aid off and on to the MPLA since 1964. It engaged in a massive campaign to arm the MPLA between August 1975 and February 1976 (when open warfare ended), which cost an estimated US$270 million. The MPLA was given such sophisticated fire-power as MIG-21s, tanks, rocket launchers, and ground-to-ground missiles (Klinghoffer, 1980:27–28). These weapons, far superior to the ones that the United States sent to its clients, would ensure victory for the Soviet-supported faction.

Effective leadership and training were obtained by the MPLA from the USSR's ally, Cuba. The permanent Cuban presence in Angola can be dated from August 1975. Havana's initial function was to train MPLA soldiers in using the weapons supplied by the Soviets. Cuban combat troops began arriving on 3 September, with large-scale deployment beginning in November after the South African assault on 23 October. The Cuban soldiers were primarily black and mulatto, making them more acceptable allies than if they had been white.

It is unclear whether Cuba's role in Angola reflected a desire to assist the revolutionary MPLA or was merely action as Moscow's proxy. The Soviet Union was instrumental in making Cuban participation possible, as it facilitated the airlifting of Cuban troops to Luanda. The USSR was likely to have favored Cuba's role, in that it allowed the Soviets to avoid direct military involvement. However, some analysts believe that Cuba responded to the crisis in Angola independently (Jackson, 1982:67–68; Klinghoffer, 1980:114). According to Jiri Valenta, "Soviet and Cuban objectives apparently coincided in Angola. It may not be far-fetched to think of the involvement in Angola rather as the action of two allies than as that of Cubans subservient to Soviet politics" (1978:25). Whichever interpretation is correct, it is certain that Cuba's participation played a decisive role in the ultimate success of Soviet policy in Angola.

Geostrategy. Among African cases, the Angola Crisis ranks high on geostrategic salience—the dominant system being involved along with the African subsystem (scale point 3). It is quite rare for the dominant system to be affected by events in Africa (only in 11.9 percent of the cases). As G. Uttley pointed out, however, Angola occupies a geographic position of considerable regional strategic significance.

> Bounded by Zaire to the north and north-east, by Zambia to the west and by Namibia to the south, Angola is in a uniquely favourable position to promote stability or instability in much of southern Africa, as has already been demonstrated by the case of SWAPO, which mounts its raids into Namibia from base camps in southern Angola, and by the invasion of Zaire's Shaba province by gendarmes operating from Angola with or without the Angolan Government's knowledge and tacit support. The potential for similar destabilizing action against Zambia is evident. (1979:24)

This statement explains in general terms why the surrounding states became entangled in the crisis.

Angola also is the transportation linchpin of southwest Africa. Zambia and Zaire are dependent on the Benguela railway to carry goods bound for export to the Atlantic coast and the deep-water harbors at Luanda and Lobito. Angola is rich in diamonds, iron ore, phosphates, gold, copper, manganese, and uranium, and the country has some oil fields. Most of these industries are dominated by Western multinationals, although none is of a scope to justify deep involvement in an extensive crisis situation.

Along the same lines, the United States has always emphasized the strategic relevance of Angola's proximity to the cape shipping route, which serves as a link between the United States and Western Europe and the Gulf. In 1975 the United States feared that, given access to Angola's deep-water ports, the Soviets could interdict oil shipments. Some analysts assert that the United States exaggerated Angola's geostrategic significance: The USSR already had access to ports in South Yemen, Mozambique, and Congo from which it could launch such actions (Klinghoffer, 1980:78; Stockwell, 1978:43). Regardless of Angola's objective geostrategic significance, the United States certainly perceived the country to be important, and this in itself was enough to involve the dominant international system in the crisis.

Heterogeneity. Angola Crisis was among the international cases from 1929 to 1979 with the highest level of heterogeneity. Military, economic, political, and cultural differences existed among the adversaries (scale point 5). This is not surprising, given the multiplicity of crisis and involved actors in Angola.

Disparities between the actors are readily observable. In terms of military capability, the superpowers are at the apex of the scale, followed by Cuba and South Africa, Zaire and Zambia, and Angola's nationalists. The economic dimension as well was dominated by the quantities of aid distributed by the superpowers. Almost every conceivable regime type was represented in the crisis, from Western democracy (United States), to Communist rule (Soviet Union, Cuba), to authoritarianism (Zaire, South Africa), to a one-party state (Zambia). Ethnic and cultural differences were prominent as well. The involved actors present in Angola came from four of the five world regions (Africa, Asia, Europe, and the Americas).

However, the cultural heterogeneity among the external actors engaged in Angola was less salient than the diversity within the African subsystem. Tribal distinctions were highly relevant in the three liberation movements. The FNLA was made up primarily of Bakongo. Upon achieving independence from Portugal, the goal of the Bakongo was to have northern Angola, their traditional territory, separated to join their ethnic brethren in southern Zaire. Needless to say, Mobutu approved this plan. The MPLA drew their rank and file from the Mbundu, the second largest ethnic group in Angola, and the urbanized, intellectual, mixed-race class. They also boasted ties with Angolan and Portuguese Marxists. UNITA, even more so than the other groups, was primarily an ethnic movement. Composed of the majority Ovimbundu, it was united by tribalism and a charismatic leader, Jonas Savimbi, rather than by ideology.

These internal ethnic cleavages had a profound effect on the crisis. They prevented the emergence of a single popular nationalist movement that would be representative of a unified Angola and capable of managing the regional dimension of the crisis. Instead, East-West and Sino-Soviet rivalries were played out through the support of rival factions. This contributed substantially to the high severity and subsequent importance of the Angola Crisis. The absence of divisive internal rivalries would have lessened the opportunities for external powers to choose sides and thus bring additional complications to the crisis.

Issues. Military-security and political-diplomatic issues were disputed during the Angola Crisis (scale point 4). Territorial jurisdiction and borders, along with the military balance in southern Africa, all had the potential to be affected by the outcome of the crisis. In addition, the distribution of influence in the region became highly unstable among both African states and external powers.

Violence. By virtually any criterion, the Angola Crisis must be regarded as a full-scale war (scale point 4). Fighting among the various factions persisted for months. Intense military engagements resulted in extensive material destruction, and casualty figures have been estimated in the thousands (Stockwell, 1978). From a more rigorous point of view, the crisis in Angola is consistent with the Correlates of War Project definition of war, a standard in aggregate research. This definition consists of two threshold conditions: (1) two or more nation-states as participants and (2) 1,000 or more battle-related casualties (Singer and Small, 1972). The Angola Crisis easily meets these conditions.

Importance

Power Change. Like most African cases, Angola concluded with a change in the relative power of adversarial actors (scale point 2). Angola itself, through the continued presence of Cuban troops, is a strong and fairly stable state, even though UNITA guerrillas continue to harrass the MPLA government. South Africa, though not weakened by its retreat from Angola, is now in a position in which it can no longer control what goes on in that state. Rather, South Africa must contend with the presence of a hostile government to the north of Namibia, which it continues to occupy.

Moscow emerged with a greater presence in southern Africa. It not only has an ally in Angola, but, more important from its standpoint, the Soviet Union was able to keep China and the United States out of this region. The United States lost ground, as Angola had been friendly territory while it was under the control of Portugal, a North Atlantic Treaty Organization (NATO) ally.

Colin Legum asserted that the balance of influence between the United States and the USSR in Africa shifted because the latter "demonstrated its willingness and capability to produce effective military support for an ally in a strategically crucial part of southern Africa. In doing so, the Russians succeeded in encouraging other liberation movements to think seriously about accepting their support" (1977:158). The United States, however, seemed determined to prevent the USSR from emerging as the sole reliable superpower ally in the minds of black African leaders. In the wake of the Angola Crisis, the United States sent US$25–30 million in security assistance to Zambia and Zaire, a US$70–75 million grant to Kenya for the purchase of a squadron on F-5E fighters, and US$50 million in arms to Zaire and planned military sales to Gabon (Crocker, 1976:666). These initiatives were expected to boost U.S. presence in the region, as well as to strengthen regimes predisposed toward pro-Western attitudes.

Actor Change. The most significant result of the crisis for Angola itself was the change in regime orientation (scale point 2). At the outset, Angola was still ruled by the Portuguese colonial regime. In compliance with the Alvor Agreement, Portugal turned over power to the people of Angola in November 1975 without recognizing any official government. This power change occurred in the midst of the fighting among the MPLA, FNLA, and UNITA.

At the conclusion of the crisis, the People's Republic of Angola had been proclaimed by the Marxist MPLA. The changes in orientation between the white colonial government and that of the black nationalists should be intuitively obvious. For example, the new leadership is hostile to the racist regime in South Africa. Furthermore, as an independent state Angola has taken a seat at the OAU, in addition to being admitted to the UN. Although the Angolan regime has relied upon the Soviet bloc for aid and arms, it also has welcomed Western multinationals seeking to do business there.

Rules Change. The Angola Crisis signaled a breakdown in consensus over intervention in African civil conflicts (scale point 3). The deployment of Cuban combat units exceeded the implicit restrictions on military involvement by non-African states in the internal affairs of the continent in its postcolonial era. To be sure, outside actors had taken military action in Africa before, as in the case of Stanleyville in 1964. The scale and persistence of Cuban involvement, however, was significantly different from previous interventions. By all accounts the troops sent by Havana had a crucial impact on the outcome of the Angola Crisis.

Alliance Change. There was no change in alliance configuration as a result of the Angola Crisis, although an MPLA-led state was recognized and admitted to the OAU on 11 February 1976, after military victory over its rivals. However, this was not an alliance change, since Angola could not be accepted into the regional organization until it achieved independence and was under the control of a recognizable government (scale point 1).

No new rifts developed between African states as a result of their alignment in the civil war. Some states, like Congo and Zaire, acted in conformity with their superpower allies. Others, like Tanzania and Zambia, acted out of regional concerns. With the disclosure that South Africa was fighting for them, the FNLA and UNITA lost considerable credibility with the rest of black Africa. Therefore, all of Africa, except for Zaire, came to recognize the MPLA as legitimate black African nationalists. Zaire, as noted, did come to recognize the MPLA, but not because of South Africa's role in the crisis.

AGGREGATE ANALYSIS

Using the weighted components of the two composite variables, the overall severity and overall importance scores for each international crisis in the period 1929–1979 period are presented in Table 29. In the light of this empirical evidence, we turn to a two-stage assessment of the Severity Index as a predictor of importance. First, the underlying general proposition that severity can predict importance will be tested by a contingency analysis. Second, to predict a specific importance score for a given case, a regression analysis will be conducted.

The results of the contingency analysis are presented in Table 30. The findings are striking and lend considerable support to the proposition that severity predicts to importance: 80.2 percent of high-severity crises scored high in importance, and 78.5 percent of low-severity crises scored low in importance. Moreover, this distribution would occur at random less than once in a thousand times.

To assess the predictive capability of the Severity Index a regression analysis was performed. Based upon the entire set of systemic crises for the period 1929–1979 (N = 189), 37 percent of the variance in importance is explained by severity. At first glance this figure is not overwhelming. However, important changes occurred at the global level during those five decades. It is our expectation that the predictive power of the Severity Index will be better in phases of global equilibrium than in phases generally regarded as transitional. The fundamental reason is that in the latter, exogeneous factors will contaminate the severity-importance linkage. In more specific terms, an international system that is disrupted by a crisis will have boundaries because it constitutes a part of the global system. The latter makes up the environment within which the systemic crisis unfolds. When the global system itself is in disequilibrium, it should be more difficult to anticipate the consequences of a systemic crisis.

The phases of equilibrium and transition can be identified as follows using the criterion of system structure:

equilibrium	1. multipolar (1929–1939)
	2. bipolarity (1948–1958)
	3. polycentrism (1963–1979)
transition	1. World War II (1939–1945)
	2. toward bipolarity (1945–1948)
	3. toward polycentrism (1959–1962)

What does the evidence on the severity-importance linkage indicate with respect to these phases of global system structure?

The findings from the regression analysis (Table 31) may be summarized as follows:

1. The predictive capability of the Severity Index is dramatically higher under equilibrium than in a transitional environment, supporting our expectation.
2. The higher levels of variance explained (68, 40, and 36 percent, respectively) apply to 38 of the 51 years under inquiry.

Improvement of the Indices of Severity and Importance is the goal of further research. Thus an examination of present shortcomings is the logical point of conclusion. It may be useful, therefore, to look more closely at some of the poorly predicted cases from the regression analysis. Current interest and limitations of space suggest that the outliers from the analysis of the polycentric system should be selected for review. The 10 crises with the largest standardized residuals are displayed in Table 32.

An inspection of the components of severity and importance for these cases reveals certain patterns. In all four cases in which severity is much higher than importance, there were no changes in either actors or rules. Although there are a number of potential explanations for this discrepancy, two possibilities will be noted here. One is that the scales for actor and rule changes should be expanded to increase their sensitivity to subtle developments that may have occurred in the crises at hand. Another explanation is that changes in rules and actors may be more difficult to bring about than had been expected.

Therefore, relatively high severity scores may not encompass all sources of instability that induce change in those dimensions.

Of the six crises in which importance exceeds severity, all but one had minimal geostrategic salience. In other words, events in "insignificant" locations nevertheless appear to have produced noteworthy long-term changes. The Bangladesh Crisis and the Rhodesian Settlement are prominent examples, in that each had a greater impact on the international system than considerations of geostrategy alone would have suggested. This finding tends to support the perspective of interdependence. The significant effects of these crises suggest the existence of a highly interconnected international system.

Further research should aim toward the improved prediction of importance on the basis of severity. Some of the scales (like those for changes in actors and rules) could be refined, perhaps through expansion. In addition, other indicators of instability should be considered. Geostrategic salience might be supplemented by connectedness. More specifically, if the actors in a crisis are more (less) connected to the general international system (in economic terms or otherwise), the effects of their interactions may be more (less) pronounced. In sum, the refinement of indicators and the incorporation of data related to interdependence would be a logical continuation to the analysis of severity and importance of systemic crisis.

TABLE 5

Number of Crisis Actors, by System

System	(Period)	1 Actor	2 Actors	3 Actors	4 Actors	5 or More Actors	Row Total
Multipolar	(1929-1939)	14 36.8	16 42.1	1 2.6	5 13.2	2.0 5.3	38 13.7
World War II	(1939-1945)	17 54.8	5 16.1	3 9.7	2 6.5	4 12.9	31 11.2
Bipolar	(1945-1962)	29 31.2	43 46.2	8 8.6	8 8.6	5 5.4	93 33.5
Polycentric	(1963-1979)	47 40.5	43 37.1	15 12.9	5 4.3	6 5.2	116 41.7
Column Total		107 38.5	107 38.5	27 9.7	20 7.2	17 6.1	278 100.0

TABLE 6

Number of Crisis Actors, by Geography

Region	1 Actor	2 Actors	3 Actors	4 Actors	5 or More Actors	Row Total
Africa	29 45.3	25 39.1	6 9.4	2 3.1	2 3.2	64 23.0
Americas	14 42.4	16 48.5	2 6.1	1 3.0	0 0	33 11.9
Asia	21 30.4	36 52.2	6 8.7	4 5.8	2 2.8	69 24.8
Europe	22 38.6	13 22.8	7 12.3	7 12.3	8 14.1	57 20.5
Middle East	21 38.2	17 30.9	6 10.9	6 10.9	5 9.1	55 19.8
Column Total	107 38.5	107 38.5	27 9.7	20 7.2	17 6.2	278 100.0

TABLE 7

Great Power Involvement, by System

System (Period)	Low Involvement			High Involvement			Row Total
	2 or More Powers Low or No Involv.	1 or More Powers High, Others Low or No Involv.	1 Crisis Actor Others Low Involv.	1 or 2 Crisis Actors, Others High or Low Involv.	2 or More Crisis Actors, Others Low or No Involv.	2 or More Crisis Actors, Others High or Low Involv.	
Multi-polar (1929-1939)	13 34.2	4 10.5	12 31.6	5 13.2	1 2.6	3 7.9	38 55.1
World War II (1939-1945)	1 3.2	6 19.4	5 16.1	17 54.8	1 3.2	1 3.2	31 44.9
Column Total	14 20.3	10 14.5	17 24.6	22 31.9	2 2.9	4 5.7	69 100.0

TABLE 8

Superpower Involvement, by System

System	(Period)	Low Involvement			High Involvement			Row Total
		2 SPs Low or No Involv.	1 SP High, 1 SP Low or No Involv.	1 SP Crisis Actor, 1 SP Low or No Involv.	2 SPs High Involv.	1 SP Crisis Actor, 1 High Crisis Involv.	2 SPs 2 SPs Crisis Actors	
Bipolar	(1945-1962)	47 50.5	16 17.2	15 16.1	1 1.1	7 7.5	7 7.5	93 44.5
Polycentric	(1963-1979)	72 62.1	15 12.9	15 12.9	6 5.2	4 3.4	4 3.4	116 55.5
Column Total		119 57.2	31 14.9	30 14.4	7 3.3	11 5.3	11 5.3	209 100.0

TABLE 9

Great Power Involvement, by Geography

Region	Low Involvement			High Involvement			Row Total
	2 or More Powers Low or No Involv.	1 or more Powers High Others Low or No Involv.	1 Crisis Actor Others Low Involv.	1 or 2 Crisis Actors, Others High or Low Involv.	2 or More Crisis Actors, Others Low or No Involv.	2 or More Crisis Actors, Others High or Low Involv.	
Africa	0 .0	0 .0	4 80.0	1 20.0	0 .0	0 .0	5 7.2
Americas	7 87.5	0 .0	1 12.5	0 .0	0 .0	0 .0	8 11.6
Asia	0 .0	2 11.8	5 29.4	9 52.9	0 .0	1 5.9	17 24.6
Europe	6 18.2	6 18.2	4 12.1	12 36.4	2 6.1	3 9.1	33 47.8
Middle East	1 16.7	2 33.3	3 50.0	0 .0	0 .0	0 .0	6 8.7
Column Total	14 20.3	10 14.5	17 24.6	22 31.9	2 2.9	4 5.8	69 100.0

TABLE 10

Superpower Involvement, by Geography

Region	Low Involvement			High Involvement			Row Total
	2 SPs Low or No Involv.	1 SP High, 1 SP Low or No Involv.	1 SP Crisis Actor, 1 SP Low or No Involv.	2 SPs High Involv.	1 SP Crisis Actor, 1 High Involv.	2 SPs Crisis Actors	
Africa	47 79.7	5 8.5	0 .0	4 6.8	1 1.7	2 3.4	59 28.2
Americas	14 56.0	5 20.0	3 12.0	0 .0	2 8.0	1 4.0	25 12.0
Asia	23 44.2	8 15.4	14 26.9	0 .0	6 11.5	1 1.9	52 24.9
Europe	6 25.0	6 25.0	9 37.5	0 .0	0 .0	3 12.5	24 11.5
Middle East	29 59.2	7 14.3	4 8.2	3 6.1	2 4.1	4 8.2	49 23.4
Column Total	119 56.9	31 14.8	30 14.4	7 3.3	11 5.3	11 5.3	209 100.0

TABLE 11

Geostrategic Salience of Crises, by System

System	(Period)	One Subsystem	Two or More Subsystems	Dominant System and One Subsystem	Dominant System and Two Subsystems	Global System	Row Total
Multipolar	(1929-1939)	22 57.9	2 5.3	9 23.7	4 10.5	1 2.6	38 13.7
World War II	(1939-1945)	7 22.6	2 6.5	11 33.5	5 16.1	6 19.4	31 11.2
Bipolar	(1945-1962)	46 49.5	22 23.7	19 20.4	3 3.2	3 3.2	93 33.5
Polycentric	(1963-1979)	86 74.1	9 7.8	18 15.5	1 .9	2 1.7	116 41.7
Column Total		161 57.9	35 12.6	57 20.5	13 4.7	12 4.3	278 100.0

TABLE 12

Geostrategic Salience of Crises, by Geography

Region	One Subsystem	Two or More Subsystems	Dominant System and One Subsystem	Dominant System and Two Subsystems	Global System	Row Total
Africa	48 75.0	9 14.1	6 9.4	1 1.6	0 .0	64 23.0
Americas	27 81.8	3 9.1	2 6.1	0 .0	1 3.0	33 11.9
Asia	32 46.4	14 20.3	20 29.0	0 .0	3 4.3	69 24.8
Europe	17 29.8	3 5.3	22 38.6	10 17.5	5 8.8	57 20.5
Middle East	37 67.3	6 10.9	7 12.7	2 3.6	3 5.5	55 19.8
Column Total	161 57.9	35 12.6	57 20.5	13 4.7	12 4.3	278 100.0

TABLE 13

Heterogeneity Among Crisis Adversaries, by System

System	(Period)	None	One Attribute	Two Attributes	Three Attributes	Four Attributes	Row Total
Multipolar	(1929-1939)	3 7.9	5 13.2	11 28.9	9 23.7	10 26.3	38 13.7
World War II	(1939-1945)	1 3.2	2 6.5	14 45.2	5 16.1	9 29.0	31 11.2
Bipolar	(1945-1962)	10 10.8	9 9.7	19 20.4	20 21.5	35 37.6	93 33.5
Polycentric	(1963-1979)	13 11.2	14 12.1	24 20.7	26 22.4	39 33.6	116 41.7
Column Total		27 9.7	30 10.8	68 24.5	60 21.6	93 33.5	278 100.0

TABLE 14

Heterogeneity Among Crisis Adversaries, by Geography

Region	None	One Attribute	Two Attributes	Three Attributes	Four Attributes	Row Total
Africa	9 14.1	4 6.3	17 26.6	15 23.4	19 29.7	64 23.0
Americas	12 36.4	8 24.2	3 9.1	3 9.1	7 21.2	33 11.9
Asia	2 2.9	5 7.2	19 27.5	8 11.6	35 50.7	69 24.8
Europe	0 .0	7 12.3	18 31.6	18 31.6	14 24.6	57 20.5
Middle East	4 7.3	6 10.9	11 20.0	16 29.1	18 32.7	55 19.8
Column Total	27 9.7	30 10.8	68 24.5	60 21.6	93 33.5	278 100.0

TABLE 15

Crisis Issues, by System

System	(Period)	One Issue Not M-S	Two Issues Not M-S	M-S Issue Alone	Two Issues Incl. M-S	Three Issues	Row Total
Multipolar	(1929-1939)	4 10.8	1 2.6	21 55.3	10 26.3	2 5.3	38 13.7
World War II	(1939-1945)	2 6.5	1 3.2	24 77.4	4 12.9	0 .0	31 11.2
Bipolar	(1945-1962)	14 15.1	8 8.6	29 31.2	35 37.6	7 7.5	93 33.5
Polycentric	(1963-1979)	15 12.9	1 .9	59 50.9	38 32.8	3 2.6	116 41.7
Column Total		35 12.6	11 4.0	133 47.8	87 31.3	12 4.3	278 100.0

TABLE 16

Crisis Issues, by Geography

Region	One Issue Not M-S	Two Issues Not M-S	M-S Issue Alone	Two Issues Incl. M-S	Three Issues	Row Total
Africa	8 12.5	1 1.6	38 59.4	15 23.4	2 3.1	64 23.0
Americas	5 15.2	2 6.1	17 51.5	7 21.2	2 6.1	33 11.9
Asia	6 8.7	1 1.4	28 40.6	32 46.4	2 2.9	69 24.8
Europe	11 19.3	3 5.3	27 47.4	11 19.3	5 8.8	57 20.5
Middle East	5 9.1	4 7.3	23 41.8	22 40.0	1 1.8	55 19.8
Column Total	35 12.6	11 4.0	133 47.8	87 31.3	12 4.3	278 100.0

TABLE 17

Violence in Crises, by System

System	(Period)	No Violence	Minor Clashes	Serious Clashes	War	Row Total
Multipolar	(1929-1939)	15 39.5	9 23.7	5 13.2	9 23.7	38 13.7
World War II	(1939-1945)	6 19.4	2 6.5	5 16.1	18 58.1	31 11.2
Bipolar	(1945-1962)	28 30.1	27 29.0	23 24.7	15 16.1	93 33.5
Polycentric	(1963-1979)	22 19.0	28 24.1	37 31.9	29 25.0	116 41.7
Column Total		71 25.5	66 23.7	70 25.2	71 25.5	278 100.0

TABLE 18

Violence in Crises, by Geography

Region	No Violence	Minor Clashes	Serious Clashes	War	Row Total
Africa	11 17.2	18 28.1	25 39.1	10 15.6	64 23.0
Americas	11 33.3	14 42.4	5 15.2	3 9.1	33 11.9
Asia	7 10.1	14 20.3	21 30.4	27 39.1	69 24.8
Europe	27 47.4	11 19.3	3 5.3	16 28.1	57 20.5
Middle East	15 27.3	9 16.4	16 29.1	15 27.3	55 19.8
Column Total	71 25.5	66 23.7	70 25.2	71 25.5	278 100.0

TABLE 19*

Severity Indicators: Rank-Order Correlation Coefficients[**]

	s_2	s_3	s_4	s_5	s_6
s_1	0.35	0.29	0.17	0.42	0.25
s_2		0.53	0.27	0.12	0.20
s_3			0.34	0.11	0.17
s_4				0.13	0.09
s_5					0.21

*N = 278, $p < 0.05$ in all cases.

**These coefficients are generated by Kendall's tau, an appropriate measure of association between variables at the ordinal level. See Table 27 for a listing of the indicators corresponding to $s_1, \ldots, s_6$.

TABLE 20[*]

Importance Indicators : Rank-Order Correlation Coefficients[**]

	i_2	i_3	i_4
i_1	0.35	0.30	0.30
i_2		0.33	0.42
i_3			0.31

[*]N = 189, $p < 0.05$ in all cases.

[**] These coefficients are generated by Kendall's tau, an appropriate measure of association between variables at the ordinal level. See Table 27 for a listing of the indicators corresponding to i_1, ... , i_4.

TABLE 21

Average Overall Severity Scores by Geography, Polarity

| Geography | Average Severity | | Percent |
	Average	Frequency	
Africa	3.31	64	23
Americas	2.97	33	12
Asia	4.35	69	25
Europe	4.73	57	20
Middle East	3.98	55	20
		———	
Total		278	
Polarity			
Multipolar (1929-39)	4.17	38	14
World War II (1939-45)	5.00	31	11
Bipolar (1945-62)	3.96	93	33
Polycentric (1963-79)	3.60	116	42
		———	
Total		278	

TABLE 22

Most Severe International Crises 1929-1979 : Time, Space, Overall Severity, Overall Importance[+]

LOCATION ** \ TIME	Africa [8.20][4.00]	Americas [7.58][5.88]	Asia [7.98][6.38]	Europe [7.90][5.78]	Middle East [8.65][15.58]
1929-39				Rhineland (1936) 7.98; 6.25 Spanish Civil War (1936-9) 8.11; 7.00 * Munich (1938) 7.44 Invasion of Albania (1939) 6.77; 4.38 Entry into World War II (1939) 10.00; 10.00 ++ [8.06][6.91]	
1939-45			Pearl Harbor (1941-2)10.00;10.00 ++ [10.00][10.00]	Invasion of Scandinavia (1940) 6.77 * Fall of Western Europe (1940) 7.04 * Balkan Invasions (1940-1) 8.65 [7.49]	
1945-62		Cuban Missiles (1962) 7.58;5.88 [7.58][5.88]	Korean War I (1950) 7.58 * Korean War II (1950-1) 8.38 * Korean War III (1953) 7.04; 7.00 Taiwan Straits II (1958) 6.91; 2.13 [7.48][4.57]	Berlin Blockade (1948-9) 7.71; 7.75 * Berlin Deadline (1957-9) 8.25; 1.75 Berlin Wall (1961) 9.32; 3.63 [8.43][4.38]	Azerbaijan (1945-6) 7.71; 4.38 Suez-Sinai (1956-7) 9.72; 5.88 Lebanon/Iraq Upheaval (1958) 6.91; 3.63 [8.11][4.63]
1963-79	Congo II (1964) 7.98; 5.50 Angola (1975-76) 9.18; 4.38 Shaba II (1978) 7.44; 2.13 [8.20][4.00]			Prague Spring (1968) 6.77; 5.50 [6.77][5.50]	Six Day War (1967) 9.72; 7.38 Yom Kippur War (1973-4) 9.18; 6.63 [9.45][7.01]

+ Each of the 26 cases in this table have an overall severity greater than 6.77.

* For an explanation of the absence of an Overall Importance score for these cases see the footnote on Table 29, pp. 11-12.

** The numbers in square brackets are the Average Overall Severity and Average Overall Importance, respectively, by region and time period.

++ The indicated Overall Importance score for this case is the score for the cluster of cases of which it was a part -- and the catalyst.

TABLE 23

Average Overall Severity of Most Severe Crises   1929-1979[*]

	Africa	Americas	Asia	Europe	Middle-East	Total Average
1929-1939				8.06		8.06
1939-1945			10.00	7.49		8.12
1945-1962		7.58	7.48	8.43	8.11	7.92
1963-1979	8.20			6.77	9.45	8.38
Total Average	8.20	7.58	7.98	7.90	8.65	

* The Total Average for a given row or column provides the average Severity
  for the cases included in that row or column.

TABLE 24

Most Severe International Crises 1929 - 1979: Components of Overall Severity

Case	Crisis Actors	Geostrategic Salience	Heterogeneity	Superpower Involvement	Issues	Violence	Overall
Remilitarization of Rhineland	6/7*	4	5	4	4	1	7.98
Spanish Civil War	4	3	5	6	4	4	8.11
Munich	4	4	3	6	4	1	7.44
Invasion of Albania	4	2	5	4	4	4	6.77
Entry to World War II	6/21*	5	5	6	3	4	10.00
Invasion of Scandinavia	5	3	3	4	3	4	6.77
Fall of Western Europe	5	3	4	4	3	4	7.04
Balkan Invasions	6	4	5	5	3	4	8.65
Pearl Harbor	6/10*	5	5	6	4	4	10.00
Azerbaijan	4	3	5	6	4	1	7.71
Berlin Blockade	4	4	4	6	4	1	7.71
Korean War I	4	3	5	5	4	4	7.58
Korean War II	5	3	5	6	3	4	8.38
Korean War III	4	5	5	3	4	4	7.04
Suez-Sinai Campaign	6	5	5	6	4	4	9.72
Berlin Deadline	5	4	4	6	4	1	8.25
Lebanon/Iraq Upheaval	4	3	5	5	2	3	6.91
Taiwan Straits II	3	3	5	5	4	3	6.91
Berlin Wall	6	4	5	6	5	1	9.32
Cuban Missiles	3	5	5	6	3	1	7.58
Congo II	4	3	5	6	4	3	7.98
Six Day War	6	5	5	6	4	4	9.72
Prague Spring	6	3	2	3	5	2	6.77
October-Yom Kippur War	5	5	5	6	4	4	9.18
Angola	6/7*	3	5	5	4	4	9.18
Shaba II	5	1	5	5	4	3	7.44

*Four international crises had more than six crisis actors: Remilitarization of the Rhineland (7), Entry into World War II (21), Pearl Harbor (10), and War in Angola (7). They are all coded 6, the highest scale point for that indicator of Severity, in order to prevent a bias toward high scores for cases with an exceptional number of participants.

TABLE 25

Most Severe International Crises   1929-1979 : Profile of Attributes

Attribute	Content	Proportion of Cases
Trigger (Breakpoint)	Violent Act	50%
Value Threat	Existence, Grave Damage, Influence	100% (42%, 31%, 27%)
Crisis Management Technique	Violence	73.1%
Centrality of Violence	Preeminent or Important	73.1%
Severity of Violence	Full-Scale War	50%
Duration	Long (61 Days+)	73.1%
Global Organization - Activity	Non-Involvement, Resolution	65.4% (34.6%, 30.8%)
Global Organization - Effectiveness	Inactive or Ineffective	73.1%
Outcome - Content	Ambiguous	73.1%
Outcome - Form	Agreement	57.9%

TABLE 26

Average Overall Importance of Most Severe Crises 1929-1979

	Africa	Americas	Asia	Europe	Middle East	Total Average
1929-1939				6.91		6.91
1939-1945			10.00			10.00
1945-1962		5.88	4.57	4.38	4.63	4.67
1963-1979	4.00			5.50	7.01	5.25
Total Average	4.00	5.88	6.38	5.78	5.58	

TABLE 27

Indices of Severity and Importance, 1973-1974 Middle East Crisis

Indicator

Severity	Weight	Assigned Score
Actors	4	5
Involvement	4	6
Geostrategy	2	5
Heterogeneity	2	5
Issues	2	4
Violence	1	4

Severity Index = $S' = 0.134 \left(\sum_{k=1}^{6} w_k s_k \right) - 1$

$= 0.134 \ (4(5) + 4(6) + 2(5) + 2(5) + 2(4) + 1(4)) - 1$

$= 9.18$

Importance	Weight	Assigned Score
Power Change	3	3
Actor Change	2	2
Rules Change	2	3
Alliance Change	1	4

Importance Index = $I' = 0.375 \left(\sum_{j=1}^{4} u_j i_j \right) - 2$

$= 0.375 \ (3(3) + 2(2) + 2(3) + 1(4)) - 2$

$= 6.63$

TABLE 28

Indices of Severity and Importance, 1975-1976 Angola Crisis

Indicator

Severity	Weight	Assigned Score
Actors	4	6
Involvement	4	6
Geostrategy	2	3
Heterogeneity	2	5
Issues	2	4
Violence	1	4

$$\text{Severity Index} = S' = 0.134 \left(\sum_{k=1}^{6} w_k s_k \right) - 1$$

$$= 0.134 \left(4(6) + 4(6) + 2(3) + 2(5) + 2(4) + 1(4) \right) - 1$$

$$= 9.18$$

Importance	Weight	Assigned Score
Power Change	3	2
Actor Change	2	2
Rules Change	2	3
Alliance Change	1	1

$$\text{Importance Index} = I' = 0.375 \left(\sum_{j=1}^{4} u_j i_j \right) - 2$$

$$= 0.375 \left(3(2) + 2(2) + 2(3) + 1(1) \right) - 2$$

$$= 4.38$$

TABLE 29

International Crises 1929-1979: Severity and Importance*

Case	Trigger Date	Overall Severity	Overall Importance
Multipolar System			
1. Chaco I	12/5/28	2.48	2.13
2. Chinese Eastern Railway	7/13/29	3.42	3.63
3. Haiti Unrest	12/4/29	3.56	4.00
4. Mukden Incident	9/18/31	5.30	5.88
5. Shanghai	1/24/32	4.76	1.75
6. Chaco II	6/18/32	2.75	3.63
7. Leticia	9/8/32	2.62	2.13
8. Jehol Campaign	2/23/33	3.56	2.13
9. Saudi-Yemen War	12/18/33	2.75	2.13
10. Austria Putsch	7/25/34	5.97	4.75
11. Assassination/King Alexander	10/9/34	2.62	2.13
12. Wal-Wal	12/6/34	4.90	--
13. Bulgaria/Turkey I	3/6/35	3.15	--
14. Kaunas Trials	3/28/35	2.89	1.00
15. Bulgaria/Turkey II	8/3/35	2.35 (3.15)	2.13
16. Ethiopan War	10/2/35	5.43	7.38
17. Maranon I	11/1/35	1.55	1.00
18. Remilitarization of Rhineland	3/7/36	7.98	6.25
19. Spanish Civil War	7/17/36	8.11	7.00
20. Alexandretta	9/9/36	4.09	2.88
21. Amur River Incident	6/22/37	3.82	--
22. Marco Polo Bridge	7/8/37	5.70	3.25

	Case	Trigger Date	Overall Severity	Overall Importance
23.	Postage Stamp Crisis	8/-/37	2.08	1.00
24.	Haiti/Dominican Republic	10/5/37	1.68	2.13
25.	Panay Incident	12/12/37	3.29	2.13
26.	Anschluss	2/12/38	4.76	7.75
27.	Polish Ultimatum	3/13/38	1.95	2.88
28.	Czech May Crisis	5/19/38	6.64	--
29.	Changkufeng Incident	7/13/38	3.96	--
30.	Munich	9/7/38	7.44	--
31.	Italian Colonial Demands	11/30/38	3.15	1.38
32.	Czech. Annexation	3/14/39	3.42 (7.44)	5.88
33.	Memel	3/15/39	2.89	--
34.	Danzig	3/21/39	2.89	2.88
35.	Invasion of Albania	3/25/39	6.77	4.38
36.	Nomonhan	5/28/39	4.09	2.50
37.	Tientsin	6/14/39	3.15	1.00
38.	Entry WWII	8/20/39	10.00	--

WWII

	Case	Trigger Date	Overall Severity	Overall Importance
39.	Soviet Occup. Baltic	9/26/39	4.23	4.75
40.	Finnish War	10/6/39	6.50	3.63
41.	Invasion of Scandinavia	4/8/40	6.77	--
42.	Fall of Western Europe	5/10/40	7.04	--
43.	Burma Road Closure	6/24/40	3.69	--
44.	Rumanian Territories	6/26/40	3.82	--
45.	Battle of Britain	7/10/40	5.16	--

	Case	Trigger Date	Overall Severity	Overall Importance
46.	East African Campaign	8/19/40	4.63	--
47.	Balkan Invasions	10/28/40	8.65	--
48.	Middle East Campaign	4/29/41	6.64	--
49.	Barbarossa	6/22/41	4.90	--
50.	Maranon II	7/5/41	1.81	--
51.	Occupation of Iran	8/25/41	4.23	--
52.	Pearl Harbor	11/26/41	10.00	--
53.	El Alamein	10/23/42	5.16	--
54.	Stalingrad	11/19/42	4.90	--
55.	Fall of Italy	7/10/43	5.97	--
56.	German Occup./Hungary	3/13/44	2.89	--
57.	Soviet Occup./East Europe	3/26/44	5.70	--
58.	D-Day	6/6/44	5.43	--
59.	Saipan	7/9/44	3.96	--
60.	Iran	9/26/44	3.42	--
61.	Leyte and Luzon	10/20/44	4.09	--
62.	Greek Civil War I	12/3/44	3.42	--
63.	Final Soviet Offensive	1/11/45	4.90 (10.00)	10.00
64.	Iwo Jima	2/19/45	4.09	--
65.	Communism in Rumania	2/24/45	3.56	--
66.	Okinawa	4/1/45	4.09	--
67.	Trieste I	5/1/45	5.30	2.13
68.	Syria/Free French Forces	5/17/45	4.76	2.13
69.	End of WWII	8/6/45	5.16 (10.00)	9.25

Case	Trigger Date	Overall Severity	Overall Importance
Bipolar System			
70. Kars-Ardahan	6/7/45	4.49	--
71. Azerbaijan	8/23/45	7.71	4.38
72. Indonesia Independence I	9/29/45	3.96	--
73. Communism in Poland	6/30/46	3.42	4.75
74. Turkish Straits	8/7/46	4.76	--
75. Greek Civil War II	11/13/46	3.56	2.88
76. Communism in Hungary	2/10/47	3.96	5.50
77. Truman Doctrine	2/21/47	5.83	3.63
78. Marshall Plan	7/4/47	3.69	--
79. Indonesia Independence II	7/21/47	4.09	--
80. Dominican Republic/Cuba	7/26/47	1.55	1.00
81. Junagadh	8/17/47	2.75	--
82. Kashmir I	10/24/47	2.75	2.88
83. Palestine Partition	11/29/47	4.09	--
84. Communism in Czechoslo-vakia	2/13/48	3.96	6.63
85. Soviet Note to Finland I	2/22/48	2.08	4.38
86. Israel Independence	5/15/48	6.24	9.25
87. Berlin Blockade	6/7/48	7.71	7.75
88. Hyderabad	8/21/48	1.95	--
89. China Civil War	9/23/48	5.43	9.25
90. CostaRica/Nicaragua I	12/11/48	1.68	2.13
91. Indonesia Independence III	12/19/48	4.09	8.13
92. Sinai Incursion	12/25/48	4.36	--

	Case	Trigger Date	Overall Severity	Overall Importance
93.	Pushtunistan I	3/-/49	3.15	2.13
94.	Luperon	6/19/49	1.68	1.75
95.	Soviet Bloc/Yugoslavia	8/19/49	2.75	3.63
96.	Korean War I	6/25/50	7.58	--
97.	Korean War II	10/1/50	8.38	--
98.	Tel Mutillah	3/15/51	3.15	2.13
99.	Punjab War Scare	7/7/51	2.35	1.00
100.	Suez Canal	7/30/51	3.96	5.13
101.	Catalina Affair	6/16/52	3.29	1.00
102.	Burma Infiltration	2/8/53	2.89	2.13
103.	Invasion of Laos I	3/24/53	4.49	4.75
104.	Korean War III	4/16/53	7.04 (8.38)	7.00
105.	East Berlin Uprising	6/17/53	2.75	3.25
106.	Trieste II	10/8/53	2.89	1.00
107.	Qibya	10/14/53	2.89	2.88
108.	Guatemala	12/12/53	6.64	4.00
109.	Dien Bien Phu	3/13/54	5.70	3.25
110.	Taiwan Straits I	8/-/54	5.83	2.88
111.	Costa Rica/Nicaragua II	1/8/55	3.02	2.13
112.	Baghdad Pact	2/24/55	2.35	3.63
113.	Gaza Raid	2/28/55	4.23	1.75
114.	Pushtunistan II	3/27/55	3.15	2.13
115.	Goa I	8/10/55	2.22	1.00
116.	Suez Nationalization	7/26/56	4.36	--

Case	Trigger Date	Overall Severity	Overall Importance
117. Qalqilya	9/13/56	3.15	2.50
118. Poland Liberalization	10/-/56	3.42	1.00
119. Hungarian Uprising	10/23/56	4.76	4.75
120. Suez/Sinai Campaign	10/29/56	9.72	5.88
121. Nicaragua/Honduras	2/26/57	2.48	1.75
122. Jordan Regime	4/4/57	1.95	3.63
123. Tunisia/France I	5/31/57	1.95	--
124. Syria/Turkey Border	8/18/57	4.76	2.50
125. Ifni	11/23/57	2.62	2.13
126. West Irian I	12/1/57	2.35	--
127. Berlin Deadline	12/15/57	8.25	1.75
128. Formation of UAR	2/1/58	1.55	5.50
129. Tunisia/France II	2/8/58	2.75	2.50
130. Sudan/Egypt Border	2/9/58	2.08	1.00
131. Indonesia-Aborted Coup	2/21/58	3.42	2.88
132. Lebanon/Iraq Upheaval	5/8/58	6.91	3.63
133. Taiwan Straits II	7/17/58	6.91	2.13
134. Cambodia/Thailand	7/24/58	3.02	1.00
135. Mexico/Guatemala Fishing Rights	12/29/58	2.48	2.13
136. Cuba/Central America I	4/25/59	4.36	--
137. India/China Border I	8/25/59	3.29	--
138. Shatt-al-Arab I	11/28/59	2.75	2.50
139. Rottem	2/15/60	2.89	2.13
140. Ghana/Togo Border	3/-/60	1.81	2.13

	Case	Trigger Date	Overall Severity	Overall Importance
141.	Assassin. Attempt - Venezuela Pres.	6/24/60	2.08	5.13
142.	Congo I: Katanga	7/5/60	3.96	3.63
143.	Mali Federation	8/20/60	2.08	4.38
144.	Cuba/Central America II	11/9/60	3.02	2.50
145.	Ethiopa/Somalia	12/26/60	2.35	1.00
146.	Pathet Lao Offensive I	3/9/61	6.37	--
147.	Bay of Pigs	4/15/61	4.76	--
148.	Pushtunistan III	5/19/61	3.42	1.00
149.	Kuwait Independence	6/25/61	3.69	1.00
150.	Bizerte	7/17/61	3.69	1.00
151.	Berlin Wall	7/29/61	9.32	3.63
152.	Vietcong Attack	9/18/61	5.70	1.38
153.	West Irian II	9/26/61	4.09	2.88
154.	Breakup of UAR	9/28/61	1.95	5.88
155.	Soviet Note to Finland II	10/30/61	2.08	1.00
156.	Goa II	12/11/61	2.22	3.25
157.	Mauritania/Mali	3/29/62	2.22	1.38
158.	Taiwan Straits III	4/22/62	2.75	1.38
159.	Pathet Lao Offensive II	5/6/62	5.30	2.88
160.	India/China Border II	9/8/62	3.82	4.00
161.	Yemen War I	9/26/62	4.90	--
162.	Cuban Missiles	10/16/62	7.58	5.88

Cases	Trigger Date	Overall Severity	Overall Importance
Polycentric System			
163. Malaysia Federation	2/11/63	2.75	3.25
164. Jordan's Internal Challenge	4/21/63	2.62	1.00
165. Dominican Republic/Haiti	4/26/63	3.15	1.75
166. Algeria/Morocco Border	10/1/63	2.62	1.00
167. Venezuela/Cuba	11/1/63	1.81	2.13
168. Kenya/Somalia	11/13/63	2.48	2.13
169. Cyprus I	11/30/63	3.96	3.25
170. Jordan Waters	12/11/63	4.23	2.13
171. Dahomey/Niger	12/21/63	2.89	1.00
172. Rwanda/Burundi	12/21/63	3.15	1.00
173. Panama Canal	1/9/64	4.36	1.38
174. East Africa Rebellions	1/19/64	2.22	2.50
175. Ogaden I	2/7/64	4.49	2.13
176. Yemen War II	5/-/64	3.82	--
177. Gulf of Tonkin	8/2/64	4.76	--
178. Congo II	8/4/64	7.98	5.50
179. Yemen War III	12/3/64	4.36	--
180. Pleiku	2/7/65	5.83	--
181. Rann of Kutch	4/8/65	2.89	--
182. Dominican Republic	4/24/65	3.29	4.38
183. Kashmir II	8/5/65	3.29	1.38
184. Guinea Regime	10/9/65	1.01	2.50
185. Rhodesia UDI	11/5/65	2.62	2.13

	Case	Trigger Date	Overall Severity	Overall Importance
186.	Yemen War IV	10/14/66	4.36 (4.90)	3.63
187.	El Samu	11/12/66	3.29	2.13
188.	Che Guevara	3/23/67	2.35	2.13
189.	Six Day War	5/18/67	9.72	7.38
190.	Cyprus II	11/15/67	3.82	3.25
191.	Pueblo	1/22/68	4.63	3.63
192.	Tet Offensive	1/30/68	6.50	--
193.	Karameh	3/18/68	3.42	3.63
194.	Prague Spring	4/9/68	6.77	5.50
195.	Essequibo Territory	7/9/68	2.35	2.50
196.	Pre-War of Attrition	9/7/68	3.96	--
197.	Beirut Airport	12/28/68	2.48	3.63
198.	Vietnam Spring Offensive	2/22/69	4.49	--
199.	Ussuri River	3/2/69	4.76	2.13
200.	War of Attrition I	3/8/69	2.75	--
201.	EC 121 Spy Plane	4/15/69	4.36	2.88
202.	Shatt-al-Arab II	4/15/69	2.62	2.13
203.	Football War	6/15/69	3.02	2.13
204.	Cairo Agreement	10/22/69	2.62	3.63
205.	War of Attrition II	1/7/70	5.70	3.63
206.	Invasion of Cambodia	3/13/70	6.50	5.88
207.	Black September	9/15/70	5.97	3.25
208.	Cienfuegos Base	9/16/70	5.30	2.88
209.	Portuguese Invasion of Guinea	11/22/70	2.62	2.13
210.	Invasion of Laos II	2/8/71	4.63	4.38

Case	Trigger Date	Overall Severity	Overall Importance
211. Bangladesh	3/25/71	4.36	6.63
212. Chad/Libya I	5/24/71	2.62	2.13
213. Caprivi Strip	10/5/71	2.75	1.00
214. Uganda/Tanzania I	10/20/71	2.75	--
215. Vietnam-Ports Mining	3/30/72	5.70	--
216. Uganda/Tanzania II	9/17/72	2.75	2.13
217. North/South Yemen I	9/26/72	2.75	1.00
218. Christmas Bombing	10/23/72	5.97	--
219. Zambia	1/19/73	2.48	1.00
220. Libyan Plane	2/21/73	3.15	2.88
221. Iraq Invasion-Kuwait	3/20/73	2.22	2.13
222. Israel Mobilization	4/10/73	2.35	--
223. Cod War	5/14/73	3.82	3.25
224. October-Yom Kippur War	10/5/73	9.18	6.63
225. South Yemen/Oman	11/18/73	2.08	2.13
226. Cyprus III	7/15/74	4.09	4.00
227. Final N. Vietnam Offensive	12/14/74	4.63 (6.50)	7.38
228. Mayaguez	5/12/75	5.30	2.13
229. War in Angola	7/12/75	9.18	4.38
230. Moroccan March-Sahara	10/16/75	3.42	--
231. Belize I	11/1/75	2.62	--
232. Sahara	11/14/75	5.57	3.25
233. Cod War II	11/23/75	1.95	1.00
234. East Timor	11/28/75	2.89	2.13

Case	Trigger Date	Overall Severity	Overall Importance
235. Lebanon Civil War I	1/18/76	2.08	--
236. Uganda Claims	2/15/76	1.81	2.13
237. Operation Thrasher	2/22/76	3.96	--
238. Nouakchott I	6/8/76	1.28	--
239. Iraqi Threat	6/9/76	1.55	1.00
240. Entebbe Raid	6/30/76	3.02	4.38
241. Sudan Coup	7/2/76	1.14	3.25
242. Aegean Sea	8/7/76	1.81	1.00
243. Nagomia Raid	8/9/76	2.48	--
244. Syria Mobilization	11/21/76	2.62	2.88
245. Operation Tangent	12/20/76	2.75	--
246. Shaba I	3/8/77	3.96	--
247. Mapai Seizure	5/29/77	2.62	--
248. Belize II	6/25/77	2.62	4.38
249. Nouakchott II	7/3/77	1.28	--
250. Libya/Egypt Border	7/14/77	2.89	1.00
251. Ogaden II	7/22/77	4.63	4.00
252. Rhodesia Raids	8/31/77	2.62	--
253. Vietnam Invasion of Cambodia	9/24/77	2.48	2.50
254. French Hostages	10/25/77	3.56	4.38
255. Chimoio Tembue Raids	11/23/77	2.62	--
256. Beagle Channel I	12/5/77	2.08	--
257. Chad/Libya II	1/22/78	2.48	--
258. Lebanon Civil War II	2/7/78	2.35	--
259. Sino/Vietnam War	2/9/78	4.09	4.75

Case	Trigger Date	Overall Severity	Overall Importance
260. Litani Operation	3/14/78	2.62	3.25
261. Cassinga Incident	5/3/78	3.96	--
262. Shaba II	5/11/78	7.44	2.13
263. Chad/Libya III	4/15/78	4.36	--
264. Air Rhodesia Incident	9/3/78	2.89	--
265. Nicaraguan Civil War	9/10/78	3.02	4.00
266. Beagle Channel II	10/16/78	2.22	1.00
267. Fall of Amin	10/30/78	4.09	4.00
268. Angola Invasion Scare	11/7/78	2.62	--
269. Tan Tan	1/28/79	1.81	--
270. Raids on ZIPRA	2/12/79	3.69	--
271. North/South Yemen II	2/24/79	4.36	1.00
272. Raids on SWAPO	3/6/79	2.75	--
273. Goulimime-Tarfaya Road	6/1/79	2.22	--
274. Soviet Threat to Pakistan	6/1/79	2.62	1.00
275. Chad/Libya IV	4/12/79	4.36	--
276. Rhodesian Settlement	7/15/79	5.30	7.00
277. Raid on Angola	10/28/79	2.75	--
278. US Hostages in Iran	11/4/79	5.16	4.00

* Of the 278 international crises in the data set, all are scored for overall severity but only 189 receive an overall importance score. The reason for the discrepancy is to be found in the existence of clusters which together act as a catalyst to change in the system. Long-war crises are a striking illustration, notably those which occurred within World War II 1939-45, Korea 1950-53, Yemen 1962-67, and Vietnam 1964-75. Unlike

severity, which measures the intensity of a crisis <u>during</u> the period of
its existence - hence a severity score for every crisis - importance gauges
the impact of a crisis several years <u>after</u> its termination. Therefore, the
consequences of each crisis within a long w a r are accurately assessed as
the impact of the entire cluster, not of any component part. For example,
the importance score for the prolonged Vietnam War is attached to the
last of the crises within that cluster, namely, Final North Vietnam Offensive
1974-75, <u>not</u> Gulf of Tonkin 1964, Tet 1968, or Spring Offensive 1969, etc.
In other words, the importance of the cluster and of each crisis within it
is gauged from the end of the Vietnam War as a whole.

There are also clusters of crises which occur in close proximity in
space and time and focus on a common issue. For example, the three India-
Pakistan crises in 1947-49, namely, Junagadh, Hyderabad and Kashmir I.
All derived from the partition of the subcontinent into two independent
states in 1947. Thus only Kashmir I, last to terminate, was given an
importance score.

While each of the 278 international crises is given an overall severity
score, as noted, a composite overall severity score for all cases in a
particular cluster is used to relate the severity of the cluster to its
overall importance. The rationale for this decision rule is as follows:
just as the overall importance score of a group of international crises
measures the greatest impact of the cluster or any case within it on the
international system, so too the overall severity of that same group of
crises should measure the greatest intensity of any case in the identical
group of crises. Wherever the severity score for the last case in a
cluster is less than the highest severity of any case therein, that highest
severity score is placed in brackets to indicate that it was the composite
overall severity score for the specific cluster; for example, the Czech
May Crisis, Munich and Czech Annexation constitute a cluster, and while
Czech Annexation was the last case in time, Munich shows the highest severity;
it is the Munich score of 7.44 which is therefore used as the composite
severity score for that cluster.

Some international crises are parts of 'unfinished' clusters, the
importance of which cannot yet be measured, such as the Lebanon Civil War
cases of 1976 and 1978, three Chad/Libya crises in 1978-79, and several
Namibia-related Angola crises in the late 1970s. The international crises
in these clusters were therefore given an empty cell for overall importance.

TABLE 30

Severity and Importance

Importance

		Low	High	
Severity	Low	73 78.5%	20 21.5%	93
	High	19 19.8%	77 80.2%	96
		92 48.7%	97 52.3%	189

$(x^2 = 65.17, df = 1, p < .001)$

* Due to the presence of tied scores, an exact division
of cases at 50% for each variable was not possible.

TABLE 31

Severity and Importance by System Structure : Results of Regression[*]

Structure	Period	Number of Cases	R	R^2	F	Significance
Stable 1 : Multipolar	1929-1939	33	.82	.68	63.0	.0001
Stable 2 : Tight Bipolarity	1948-1958	42	.64	.40	25.1	.0001
Stable 3 : Polycentrism	1963-1979	79	.60	.36	42.3	.0001
Transition 1 : to Bipolarity	1945-1948	10	.46	.21	11.9	.0013
Transition 2 : to Polycentrism	1959-1962	25				

* Due to the small N's for the Transition, these periods have been combined for purposes of this analysis.

TABLE 32

Polycentric System: Outliers from Regression Analysis

Systemic Crisis	Severity	Importance	Standardized Residual
Panama Canal	4.36	1.38	-1.52
Bangladesh	4.36	6.63	2.48
Final N. Vietnamese Off.	4.36	7.38	2.95
Mayaguez	5.30	2.13	-1.32
Nouakchott II	1.28	4.00	1.73
French Hostages	3.56	4.38	1.47
Sino/Vietnam War	4.09	4.75	2.11
Shaba II	7.44	2.13	-1.91
North/South Yemen II	4.36	1.00	-1.81
Rhodesian Settlement	5.30	7.00	2.38

Epilogue

It is reasonable to conclude that the central postulate of the Crisis-as-Earthquake Model—a meaningful association between Severity and Importance—is supported by the evidence from five decades of international crises in the twentieth century. The ultimate test will be the accuracy of estimates about the likely importance of future crises.[41] Whatever the results, we now have an empirically tested method to measure the impact of crises as international political earthquakes.

The similarity between an Index of Severity to measure political upheavals and the Richter scale to measure geological tremors should now be apparent. We have devised and applied a scale that measures the consequences of crises for the political structure of international systems. In short, crises viewed as earthquakes not only act as catalysts to system change. The concepts of severity and importance of crises also provide a fruitful path to assess the content and extent of system change.

Notes

1. See, for example, Buzan and Jones (1981); Gilpin (1981); Haas (1983); Holsti et al. (1980); Keohane and Nye (1977); Mansbach and Vasquez (1981); Olson (1982); Ruggie (1982, 1983); Vasquez and Mansbach (1983); Waltz (1979); Young (1982). For the reasons for the relative neglect of change, see Gilpin (1981:4–6).

2. A data set on international crises from 1929 to 1979 has been generated to facilitate the achievement of some of these goals (see Table 29). The procedures for determining comprehensiveness of cases and encoding variables are explained in a forthcoming handbook prepared by Brecher, Wilkenfeld, and Moser (1987). The data used in the present study, along with an abridged codebook, will be available from the Inter-University Consortium on Political Research.

3. In 1945 there were 51 members of the UN. By 1960 this number had increased to 100 members. And in 1985 there are 159 members.

4. Although not identical, these strands are similar to Singer's (1971:8, 9) two major usages of the system concept in the social sciences—system of entity and system of action.

5. In the literature on systems, though not that on international systems, process is also used to denote growth and decay, concepts closely linked to system transformation. The latter, though not the central focus of this book, will be discussed in relation to stability and equilibrium.

6. The concept of ultrastable system was developed by Ashby (1952:100–122). The international system has been characterized by continuity amid change over the centuries. It is ultrastable since it maintained the basic feature of anarchy and power hierarchy, that is, the absence of universal empire or world government despite multiple significant shifts in both equilibrium and stability.

7. Michael Haas's treatise on international conflict (1974), for example, has an appendix on "Definitions of Concepts" of 23 pages, in which equilibrium is conspicuously absent.

8. A crisis defined here refers to the military-security (war-peace) issue-area. However, breakpoints may occur in any foreign policy issue, and the study of international political, economic, and status crises might yield no less valuable findings. For these types an appropriate change is necessary in the second condition specified.

9. At the system level, however, there is no component corresponding to finite time for response. Time is built into the concepts of severity and importance during and after a crisis. Time is therefore relevant to, but is not a necessary condition of, a systemic crisis, unlike "finite time"—the awareness by decisionmakers of the constraints on their response to perceived threat, in a definition of crisis at the unit (actor level. At the macro (system) level, time does not have an analogous function. It merely designates the duration of an international crisis, from the first breakpoint event (a disturbance to the system) in the form of a trigger to a crisis for one or several states, to the final exitpoint, which (in the current data set) denotes a significant reduction in conflictual activity within the system. Illustrations of the onset of an international crisis are the Soviet-supported attempt by the Tudeh party on 23 August 1945 to take over the Azerbaijan capital of Tabriz, the beginning of the Azerbaijan Crisis; the crossing of the Thag La Ridge in the North East Frontier Agency by Chinese forces on 8 September 1962, setting in motion the Sino-Indian border crisis; and the dispatch of additional Egyptian forces into Sinai as well as an overflight of Israel's nuclear research center in the Negev, on 17 May 1967, leading to a major Arab-Israeli crisis. These crises ended, respectively, with the withdrawal of Soviet troops from Iran on 9 May 1945, the unilateral declaration of a cease-fire by Beijing on 1 December 1962, and the end of the Six Day War on 11 June 1967. Thus time is relevant to, but not a necessary condition of, a systemic crisis. The conceptual linkages noted here are elaborated in Brecher and Ben Yehuda (1985).

10. This is not true, however, for intra-war crises (IWC), that is, situational changes during a war that trigger a perception of threat and time pressure for decision, and, as a replacement for war likelihood, a perception of adverse change in the military balance. For a discussion of indicators of intra-war crises see Brecher (1977:45).

11. A crisis was triggered for Pakistan on 8 April 1965 when India launched an attack on the disputed Kutch border. The Pakistani response, a counterattack on the same day, triggered a crisis for India. The unit-level crises were transformed instantly into a systemic crisis.

12. The crisis trigger for Belgium, on 5 July 1960, was a mutiny among soldiers of the Congolese Force Publique, which rapidly turned into a general movement against Belgian and other European residents. Belgium responded on 8 July by announcing its intention to send military reinforcements to the Congo. A crisis was triggered for the Congo two days later when Belgian troops went into action.

13. The Missile Crisis for the United States was triggered on 16 October 1962 when photographic evidence was presented to President John F. Kennedy showing the presence of Soviet missiles in Cuba. The U.S. major response, on 22 October, was a decision to blockade all offensive military equipment en route to Cuba. The blockade in turn triggered unit-level crises for the Soviet Union and Cuba.

14. All systemic breakpoints constitute escalation points in unit-level crises, but the reverse does not hold true; there may be, and usually are, escalation

points during a crisis for a state other than the internal triggering event leading to its first perception of threat, time pressure, and war likelihood.

15. To engage in reliable anticipation it will be necessary to establish the severity configuration early in a future international crisis. Some indicators will be evident at the outset, such as crisis actors and issues. Some, including these, may undergo change during a crisis, such as the extent of superpower involvement. This can be tested by comparing the configuration of severity at the outset and at the conclusion of past crises.

16. The choice of a limited set of indicators derives from the conviction that it is necessary to strike a balance between economy and exhaustiveness. Intercoder reliability for this set of indicators was over 95 percent.

17. There are systemic crises with only one crisis actor, that is, a state that perceives for itself a threat to one or more basic values, finite time for response, and the likelihood of involvement in military hostilities before the threatening situational change is overcome—the three components of a crisis at the unit level. However, every crisis actor has at least one adversary, usually the state that triggers its crisis. It is disruptive interactions between these adversaries, whether two (or more) crisis actors or one crisis actor and one noncrisis actor, that meet the first condition of a systemic crisis.

18. For a rank order of states from 1950 to 1967 according to power see Cox and Jacobson (1974).

19. This expectation accords with the findings from the abundant literature on cross-cutting cleavages in domestic politics. Case studies indicate that the multiple cleavages among competing interest groups make political accommodation more difficult; that is, they are reinforcing cleavages. For example, the splits between Protestants and Roman Catholics in Northern Ireland, Christians and Muslims in Lebanon, French- and English-speaking communities in Quebec are accentuated by other cleavages, notably education, income, urbanization, and so on. The cleavages, in our terms, are characterized as multiple heterogeneity. On the effects of cross-cutting cleavages or their absence see Lijphart (1968), Lipset (1960), and Rose (1980).

20. Intercoder reliability for this set of indicators was over 90 percent.

21. A change in the relative power of adversaries is identified with any one of the following combinations of crisis outcomes as perceived by a specific crisis actor (e.g., United States or USSR or Cuba in the 1962 Missile Crisis): victory-defeat; victory-stalemate; victory-compromise; stalemate-defeat; compromise-stalemate; compromise-defeat. No change in relative power is indicated when the adversaries in a systemic crisis perceived an identical outcome, such as victory-victory, compromise-compromise, and so on.

22. The concept of stability in international politics generally will be elaborated in a forthcoming paper by Brecher and James on "Stability and Polarity: A 'Great Debate' Revisited."

23. To preserve the clarity of the Severity Index as a predictive mechanism no effort will be made to incorporate the indirect linkages that may exist. Even the inclusion of linkages with only one intervening indicator would require the analysis of an additional 120 possibilities.

24. In formal terms:

$$S = \sum_{k=1}^{6} w_k s_k$$

Where S = Severity Index; s_k = kth indicator ($k = 1, \ldots, 6$); and w_k = weight assigned to kth indicator.

25. The calculation for number of dyads (D) is performed as follows:

$$D = f(n)$$
$$= \frac{n(n-1)}{2}$$

26. Crisis participants interacting with superpowers face an obvious constraint: The superpowers are capable of responding severely. In fact, acts of violence directed toward the superpowers actually have been inflicted on client states.

27. For other potential crisis actors a threshold of distance, which is expected to vary from one state to another, may exist beyond which even very high geostrategic salience will not induce involvement.

Any connection between geostrategic salience and the number of issues would be indirect; since more actors are likely to participate in strategically located crises, more issues may be expected as well. There is no reason to expect a direct linkage; in fact, some areas may even be crucial because control over them would provide a virtual monopoly over some single resource. Or, it could be the case that a location that is moderately important in several ways also has the potential to evoke high salience. Both arguments seem plausible.

There is no clear basis for expecting the level of violence in a crisis to be influenced by geostrategy. On one hand, those active in a highly sensitive region might be inclined toward prudence in the use of force because of the danger of escalation. On the other hand, they might be more apt to resort to violence to achieve goals. A parallel analysis could easily be presented for geostrategically remote locations.

28. There is no direct linkage between geostrategic salience and heterogeneity. Arguably, since geostrategy affects the number of actors, which in turn promotes heterogeneity, indicator s_3 affects heterogeneity indirectly. (But to reiterate, such indirect linkages will not be included in the derivation of weights for the Index of Severity.)

29. Heterogeneity may be linked indirectly to superpower involvement because both are affected similarly by the number of actors. It is hard to imagine why similarity (or diversity) among parties to a crisis in and of itself would induce (or inhibit) superpower activity. Similarly, it is not expected to have an impact on the number of actors. Instead, as indicated, a larger number of actors will lead to greater diversity.

30. There is no reason to expect the number of issues to affect the level of violence. A single-issue crisis might cause those involved to focus more intensely on their divergent preferences over that issue, with violence as the

outcome. It is also possible that conflict across a range of subject areas could indicate a more pervasive degree of conflict, with the result being violent crisis management. It is unclear which possibility (if either) should take precedence.

31. Violence is not expected to have an impact on the number of actors. In some cases it may have a cathartic effect: Once it occurs, the intensity of the crisis subsides and as a result uninvolved states stay that way. Under other circumstances violence may exacerbate existing strife and trigger crises for some of those outside the current boundaries of the conflict.

Heterogeneity, too, is independent of violent crisis management. In fact, the causal linkage is in the other direction. It might be conjectured that violent crises will promote heterogeneity because interactions of such intensity could arouse interest among rather diverse outside observers. But the violence also could be the result of intense disagreement over a specific substantive point, with interested parties on the outside sharing certain characteristics associated with concern over that issue. Since arguments can be made either way, there is no justification for linking heterogeneity with violence.

Violence is not linked to issues. The arguments here are much the same as those offered for the case of violence and its potential to produce heterogeneity. On one hand, violence might raise new issues and expand the domain of conflict. On the other, it could focus attention more directly on a single issue as the cause of the crisis.

32. Formally,

$$I = \sum_{j=1}^{4} u_j i_j$$

where I = Importance Index; i_j = jth indicator (j = 1, . . . , 4); and u_j = weight assigned to jth indicator.

33. Actors are not expected to affect the rules of the game that, in general, are relatively static. Couched as self-defense, resort to violence is nearly universal and always has been. Fluctuations in specific attributes of system members ordinarily will not produce different behavioral norms.

34. Rules do not affect power; they reflect it. As indicated, societal norms derive from the existence of some type of enforcement mechanism, although a degree of conformity may exist even in the absence of coercive power. In a state of anarchy, authority generally rests with the most powerful.

35. Changes in alliances occur as a result of actor changes, not the reverse. A state's regime does not change as a function of its coalitional affiliations, nor do actors leave or enter the system because of alliance commitments. Hence the linkage of actors with alliances is ruled out on logical grounds.

Changing alliance configurations are also not expected to affect the rules of the game. As indicated previously, systemic norms are insensitive to short-term disruptions. Even a completely new system of alliances would not necessarily indicate a new set of rules. The system may undergo severe coalitional gyrations and yet remain essentially anarchical.

36. This analysis does not include temporal and regional breakdowns for the indicators of importance. The severity data are "hard" by comparison, and it would be inappropriate to conduct the same kind of descriptive analysis for the "soft" importance figures.

37. For a comparison of crises encompassed by protracted conflicts with those that are not, see Brecher (1984).

38. The linear equations used to transform the scales are as follows, with S' and I' representing the transformed scores.

$$S' = 0.134(S) - 1$$
$$I' = 0.375(I) - 2$$

39. The following exposition is based upon Aruri 1975; Bandmann and Cordova 1980; Bartov 1978; Brecher 1980; Dayan 1976; Dowty 1984; Eban 1977; Freedman 1975; G. Golan 1974, 1977; M. Golan 1976; Heikal 1975; Herzog 1975; Kalb and Kalb 1974; Kissinger 1982; Meir 1975; Monroe and Farrar-Hockley 1975; Nixon 1978; Quandt 1977; Sadat 1978; Schiff 1975; Shimoni 1977.

40. To permit a statistical analysis it is essential to select specific break-points. It is recognized, however, that the crises that have been designated as points of transition are only the most salient by comparison to other reasonable choices within an approximate time period. These crises should not be regarded as the exclusive agents of global disequilibrium or the return to an equilibrium state. The breakpoints are as follows: from the multipolar system to World War II, following the case Entry into World War II; from embryonic to tight bipolarity, beginning with the Czechoslovakia Crisis of 1948 leading to its entry into the Soviet bloc; from tight bipolarity to a transitional phase commonly termed "loose bipolarity," starting with the Taiwan Straits Crisis of 1958, marking the PRC's open break with the Soviet Union and, in the Western bloc, the beginning of military withdrawal from NATO by the French under Charles de Gaulle; and the emergence of polycentrism following the Cuban Missile Crisis and the Sino-Indian Border War at the end of 1962.

41. The intention is to apply the predictive mechanism for a polycentric structure to a set of case studies in the post-1979 era.

References

Aron, R. (1966). *Peace and War*. Garden City, N.Y.: Doubleday.

―――― (1957). In *The Nature of Conflict*, pp. 177–203. Paris: UNESCO.

Arrow, K. J. (1968). "Economic Equilibrium," in David L. Sills ed., *International Encyclopedia of the Social Sciences*, vol. 4, pp. 367–389. New York: Macmillan and Free Press.

Aruri, Nasser H., ed. (1975). *Middle East Crucible: Studies on the Arab-Israeli War of October 1973*. Wilmette, Ill.: Medina University Press International.

Ashby, W. R. (1952). *Design for a Brain: The Origin of Adaptive Behavior*. New York: Wiley.

Azar, E. E. (1975). "Ten Issues in Events Research." In Azar and Joseph D. Ben-Dak, eds., *Theory and Practice of Events Research*, pp. 1–17. New York: Gordon and Breach.

―――― (1972). "Conflict Escalation and Conflict Reduction in an International Crisis: Suez, 1956." *Journal of Conflict Resolution* (June) 16:183–201.

―――― , R. Brody, and C. A. McClelland (1972). "International Events Interactions Analysis: Some Research Considerations." Beverly Hills, Calif.: Sage Professional Papers in International Studies, 02-001.

―――― , R. D. McLaurin, Thomas Havener, Craig Murphy, Thomas Sloan, and Charles H. Wagner (1977). "A System for Forecasting Crisis: Findings and Speculations about Conflict in the Middle East." *International Interactions* 3:193–225.

Bandmann, Yona, and Yishai Cordova (1980). "The Soviet Nuclear Threat Towards the Close of the Yom Kippur War." *Jerusalem Journal of International Relations* 5, 1:94–110.

Bartov, Hanoch (1978). *Dado: Forty Eight Years and Another Twenty Days*, 2 vols. Tel Aviv: Ma'ariv Library (Hebrew).

Binder, L. (1958). "The Middle East as a Subordinate International System." *World Politics* (April) 10:408–429.

Boals, K. (1973). "The Concept 'Subordinate International System': A Critique." In Richard A. Falk and Saul H. Mendlovitz eds., *Regional Politics and World Order*, pp. 399–411. San Francisco: W. H. Freeman.

Boulding, K. E. (1956). "General Systems Theory—The Skeleton of Science." *Management Science* (April) 2:147–208.

Bowman, L. W. (1968). "The Subordinate State System of Southern Africa." *International Studies Quarterly* (September) 12:231–261.

141

Brecher, Michael (1984). "International Crises and Protracted Conflicts." *International Interactions* 11:237–297.

———— (1980). *Decisions in Crisis: Israel, 1967 and 1973.* Berkeley and Los Angeles: University of California Press.

———— (1978). "A Theoretical Approach to International Crisis Behavior." *Jerusalem Journal of International Relations* (Winter-Spring) 3:5–24.

———— (1963). "International Relations and Asian Studies: The Subordinate State System of Southern Asia." *World Politics* (January) 15:213–235.

———— and H. Ben Yehuda (1985). "System and Crisis in International Politics." *Review of International Studies* (January) 11, 1:17–36.

————, J. Wilkenfeld, and S. Moser. *Handbook on International Crises.* Berkeley and Los Angeles: University of California Press, forthcoming.

Burgess, P. M., and R. W. Lawton (1972). *Indicators of International Behaviour: An Assessment of Events Data Research.* Beverly Hills, Calif.: Sage Professional Papers, International Studies Series, vol. 1.

Buzan, B., and R.J.B. Jones, eds. (1981). *Change and the Study of International Relations: The Evaded Dimension.* London: Frances Pinter.

Cantori, L. J., and S. J. Spiegel (1970). *International Politics of Regions.* Englewood Cliffs, N.J.: Prentice-Hall.

Corson, W. H. (1970). *Conflict and Cooperation in East-West Crises.* Ph.D. dissertation, Harvard.

Cox, R. W., and H. K. Jacobson (1974). *The Anatomy of Influence.* New Haven: Yale University Press.

Crocker, C. A. (1976). "The African Dimension of Indian Ocean Policy." *Orbis* 20 (Fall):637–667.

Dayan, Moshe (1976). *Story of My Life.* Jerusalem and Tel Aviv: Steimatzky's Agency.

Dean, P. D., and J. A. Vasquez (1976). "From Power Politics to Issue Politics." *Western Political Quarterly* 29:7–28.

Deutsch, K. W. (1974). *Politics and Government,* 2d ed. Boston: Houghton Mifflin.

———— and J. D. Singer (1964). "Multipolar Power Systems and International Stability." *World Politics* (April) 16:390–406.

Dominguez, J. E. (1971). "Mice that Do not Roar." *International Organization* (Spring) 25:175–208.

Dowty, Alan (1984). *Middle East Crisis: US Decision-Making in 1958, 1970 and 1973.* Berkeley and Los Angeles: University of California Press.

East, M. A., S. A. Salmore, and C. F. Hermann (1978). *Why Nations Act.* Beverly Hills, Calif., London: Sage.

Eban, Abba (1977). *An Autobiography.* Jerusalem and Tel Aviv: Steimatzky's Agency.

Eckhardt, W., and E. E. Azar (1978). "Major World Conflict and Interventions, 1945–1975." *International Interactions* 5, 1:75–110.

Forrester, J. W. (1973). *World Dynamics,* 2d ed. Cambridge: Wright-Allen Press.

Freedman, Robert O. (1975). *Soviet Policy Towards the Middle East since 1970.* New York: Praeger.

Friedman, M. (1953). *Essays in Positive Economics*. Chicago and London: University of Chicago Press.

Gilpin, R. (1981). *War and Change in World Politics*. New York: Cambridge University Press.

Golan, Galia (1977). *Yom Kippur and After: The Soviet Union and the Middle East Crisis*. Cambridge: Cambridge University Press.

_____ (1974). *The Soviet Union and the Arab-Israel War of October 1973*. Jerusalem Papers on Peace Problems, no. 7. Jerusalem: Hebrew University Leonard Davis Institute for International Relations.

Golan, Matti (1976). *The Secret Conversations of Henry Kissinger: Step-by-Step Diplomacy in the Middle East*. New York: Bantam Books.

Haas, E. B. (1983). "Regime Decay: Conflict Management and International Organizations, 1945–1981." *International Organization* (Spring) 37:189–256.

_____ (1970). "The Study of Regional Integration." *International Organization* (Autumn) 24:607–646.

_____ (1964). *Beyond the Nation State*. Stanford: Stanford University Press.

Haas, M. (1974). *International Conflict*. Indianapolis: Bobbs-Merrill.

_____ (1970). "International Subsystems: Stability and Polarity." *American Political Science Review* (March) 64:98–123.

Hanrieder, W. F. (1965). "The International System: Bipolar or Multibloc?" *Journal of Conflict Resolution* (September) 9:229–307.

Heikal, Mohamed (1975). *The Road to Ramadan*. London: Collins.

Hellmann, D. C. (1969). "The Emergence of an East Asian International Subsystem." *International Studies Quarterly* (December) 13:421–434.

Hermann, C. F., ed. (1972). *International Crises: Insights from Behavioral Research*. New York: Free Press.

Herzog, Chaim (1975). *The War of Atonement*. London: Weidenfeld & Nicholson.

Hoffmann, S. (1963). "Discord in Community." *International Organization* (Summer) 17:521–549.

_____ (1961). "International Systems and International Law." *World Politics* (October) 14:205–237.

Holsti, K. J. (1972). *International Politics*, 2d ed. Englewood Cliffs, N.J.: Prentice-Hall.

Holsti, O. R., R. M. Siverson, and A. L. George, eds. (1980). *Change in the International System*. Boulder, Colo.: Westview Press.

Jackson, H. F. (1982). *From the Congo to Soweto: US Foreign Policy Toward Africa Since 1960*. New York: William Morrow.

Kaiser, K. (1968). "The Interaction of Regional Subsystems." *World Politics* (October) 21:84–107.

Kalb, Marvin, and Bernard Kalb (1974). *Kissinger*. Boston: Little, Brown.

Kaplan, M. A. (1957). *System and Process in International Politics*. New York: Wiley.

Katzenstein, P. J. (1975). "International Interdependence: Some Long Term Trends and Recent Changes." *International Organization* (Autumn) 29:1021–1034.

Keohane, R. O. (1981). Letter to one of the authors.

———— and J. S. Nye (1977). *Power and Interdependence.* Boston: Little, Brown.

Kissinger, Henry A. (1982). *Years of Upheaval.* London: Weidenfeld & Nicholson.

Klinghoffer, Arthur Jay (1980). *The Angolan War: A Study in Soviet Policy in the Third World.* Boulder, Colo.: Westview Press.

Lampert, D. E. (1980). "Patterns of Transregional Relations." In Werner J. Feld and Gavin Boyd, eds., *Comparative Regional Systems,* pp. 129–481. New York: Pergamon Press.

Legum, Colin (1977). "The Soviet Union, China and the West in Southern Africa." In Steven L. Spiegel, ed., *At Issue: Politics in the World Arena,* 2d ed. New York: St. Martin's Press.

Lijphart, A. (1968). *The Politics of Accommodation: Pluralism and Democracy in the Netherlands.* Berkeley and Los Angeles: University of California Press.

Lipset, S. M. (1960). *Political Man.* Garden City, N.Y.: Doubleday.

Liska, G. (1957). *International Equilibrium.* Cambridge: Harvard University Press.

McClelland, C. A. (1972). "Comments." In C. Hermann, ed., *International Crises,* pp. 6–7. New York: Free Press.

———— (1968). "Access to Berlin: The Quantity and Variety of Events, 1948–1963." In J. D. Singer, ed., *Quantitative International Politics: Insights and Evidence,* pp. 159–186. New York: Free Press.

———— (1966). *Theory and International System.* New York: Macmillan.

———— (1964). "Action Structures and Communication in Two International Crises: Quemoy and Berlin." *Background* 7:201–215.

———— (1958). "Systems and History in International Relations: Some Perspectives for Empirical Research and Theory." In *General Systems, Yearbook of the Society for General Systems Research,* vol. 3, pp. 221–247. Ann Arbor, Mich.: Society for General Systems Research.

———— (1955). "Applications of General Systems Theory in International Relations." *Main Currents in Modern Thought* (November) 12:27–34.

McCormick, J. M. (1978). "International Crises: A Note on Definition," *Western Political Quarterly* 31:352–358.

Mansbach, R. W., and J. A. Vasquez (1981). *In Search of Theory: A New Paradigm for Global Politics.* New York: Columbia University Press.

Marcum, John A. (1978). *The Angolan Revolution.* Vol. 2: *Exile Politics and Guerrilla Warfare (1962–1976).* Cambridge, Mass.: MIT Press.

———— (1976). "Lessons of Angola." *Foreign Affairs* 54 (April) 54: 407–425.

Meadows, D. H. et al. (1972). *The Limits to Growth.* New York: Universe Books.

Meir, Golda (1975). *My Life.* Jerusalem and Tel Aviv: Steimatzky's Agency.

Modelski, G. (1961). "International Relations and Area Studies: The Case of Southeast Asia." *International Relations* (April) 2:143–155.

Monroe, Elizabeth, and A. H. Farrar-Hockley (1975). *The Arab-Israel War, October 1973—Background and Events.* Adelphi Papers III. London: International Institute for Strategic Studies.

Moore, W. E. (1968). "Social Changes." In D. L. Sills, ed., *International Encyclopedia of the Social Sciences*, vol. 14, pp. 365–375. New York: Free Press.

Nixon, Richard M. (1978). *RN: The Memoirs of Richard Nixon*. New York: Grosset & Dunlop.

Olson, M. (1982). *The Rise and Decline of Nations: Economic Growth, Stagflation and Social Rigidities*. New Haven: Yale University Press.

Peterson, S. (1975). "Research on Research: Events Data Studies, 1961–1972." In Patrick J. McGowan, ed., *Sage International Yearbook of Foreign Policy Studies*, vol. 3. Beverly Hills, Calif.: Sage.

Potter, W. C. (1980). "Issue-Area and Foreign Policy Analysis." *International Organization* (Summer) 34:405–427.

Pruitt, D. G. (1969). "Stability and Sudden Change in Interpersonal and International Affairs." *Journal of Conflict Resolution* (March) 13:18–38.

Quandt, William B. (1977). *Decade of Decisions: American Policy Toward the Arab-Israeli Conflict 1967–1976*. Berkeley and Los Angeles: University of California Press.

Rose, R., ed. (1980). *Challenge to Governance*. Beverly Hills, Calif.: Sage.

Rosecrance, R. N. (1966). "Bipolarity, Multipolarity, and the Future." *Journal of Conflict Resolution* 10:314–327.

_____ (1963). *Action and Reaction in World Politics: International Systems in Perspective*. Boston: Little, Brown.

Rosenau, J. N. (1972). In J. N. Rosenau, V. Davis, and M. East, eds., *The Analysis of International Politics*, pp. 145–165. New York: Free Press.

_____ (1966). "Pre-Theories and Theories of Foreign Policy." In R. Barry Farrell, ed., *Approaches to Comparative and International Politics*, pp. 27–92. Evanston, Ill.: Northwestern University Press.

_____ (1963). "The Functioning of International Systems." *Background* (November) 7:115, fn. 4.

Ruggie, J. S. (1983). "Continuity and Transformation in the World Polity: Toward a Neorealist Synthesis." *World Politics* (January) 35:261–285.

_____ (1982). "International Regimes, Transactions and Change: Embedded Liberalism in the Postwar Economic Order." *International Organization* 36:379–416.

Russett, B. M. (1967). *International Regions and the International System*. Chicago: Rand McNally.

Sadat, Anwar (1978). *In Search of Identity: An Autobiography*. New York: Harper & Row.

Schiff, Zeev (1975). "The Full Story of the Encirclement that Ended the Yom Kippur War." *Haaretz*, 14 September 1975 (Hebrew).

Shepherd, G. W. (1970). *Nonaligned Black Africa: An International Subsystem*. Lexington, Mass.: Heath.

Shimoni, Yaacov (1977). *The Arab States*. Tel Aviv: Am Oved (Hebrew).

Singer, J. D. (1971). *A General Systems Taxonomy for Political Science*. New York: General Learning Press.

_____ (1961). "The Level-of-Analysis Problem in International Relations." *World Politics* (October) 14:77–92.

————— and M. Small (1972). *The Wages of War, 1816–1965: A Statistical Handbook.* New York: Wiley.

Stockwell, John (1978). *In Search of Enemies: A CIA Story.* New York: Norton.

Tanter, R. (1978). "International Crisis Behavior: An Appraisal of the Literature." *Jerusalem Journal of International Relations* (Winter-Spring) 3:340–374.

————— (1975). "Crisis Management: A Critical Review of Academic Literature." *Jerusalem Journal of International Relations* (JJIR) 1:71–101.

————— (1974). *Modelling and Managing International Conflicts: The Berlin Crises.* Beverly Hills, Calif.: Sage Library of Social Research, 6.

————— (1966). "Dimensions of Conflict Behavior Within and Between Nations, 1958–1960." *Journal of Conflict Resolution* 10:41–64.

Thompson, W. R. (1981). "Center-Periphery Interaction Patterns: The Case of Arab Visits, 1946–1975." *International Organization* (Spring) 35:355–373.

————— (1973). "The Regional Subsystem." *International Studies Quarterly* (March) 17:89–117.

————— (1970). "The Arab Sub-System and the Feudal Pattern of Interaction: 1965." *Journal of Peace Research* 2, 2:151–167.

Uttley, Garrick (1979). "Globalism or Regionalism? United States Policy Towards Southern Africa." *Adelphi Papers No. 154.* London: International Institute for Strategic Studies.

Valenta, Jiri (1978). "The Soviet-Cuban Intervention in Angola, 1975." *Studies in Comparative Communism* 11 (Spring-Summer):3–33.

Vasquez, J. A., and R. W. Mansbach (1983). "The Issue Cycle: Conceptualizing Long-Term Global Political Change." *International Organization* (Spring) 3:257–279.

Waltz, K. N. (1979). *Theory of International Politics.* Reading, Mass.: Addison-Wesley.

————— (1967). "International Structure, National Force, and the Balance of World Power." *Journal of International Affairs* 21, 2:215–231.

————— (1964). "The Stability of a Bipolar World." *Daedalus* (Summer) 93:881–909.

————— (1959). *Man, the State and War.* New York: Columbia University Press.

Wiener, A. M. and H. Kahn, eds., (1962). *Crisis and Arms Control.* New York: Hudson-Institute.

Wilkenfeld, J., Virginia Lee Lussier, and Dale Tahtinen (1972). "Conflict Interactions in the Middle East, 1949–1967." *Journal of Conflict Resolution* (June) 16:135–154.

Wilkenfeld, Jonathan, and Michael Brecher (1982). "Superpower Crisis Management Behaviour." In Charles W. Kegley, Jr., and Pat McGowan, eds., *Sage International Yearbook of Foreign Policy Studies. Vol. 7: Foreign Policy USA/USSR.* Beverly Hills, Calif.: Sage.

Yalem, J. (1970). *Regional Subsystems and World Politics.* Tucson, Ariz.: University of Arizona, Institute of Government Research, 4.

Young, O. R. (1982). "Regime Dynamics: The Rise and Fall of International Regimes." *International Organization* (Spring) 36:277–298.

———— (1968a). *A Systemic Approach to International Politics*. Princeton, N.J.: Center of International Studies, Princeton University.

———— (1968b). "Political Discontinuities in the International System." *World Politics* (April) 20:369–392.

———— (1968c). *The Politics of Force*. Princeton, N.J.: Princeton University Press.

Zartman, I. W. (1967). "Africa as a Subordinate State System in International Relations." *International Organization* (Summer) 21:545–564.

Zimmerman, W. (1972). "Hierarchical Regional Subsystems and the Politics of System Boundaries." *International Organization* (Winter) 26:18–26.

Zinnes, D. A. (1980). "Prerequisites for the Study of System Transformation." In O. R. Holsti, A. L. George, and R. M. Siverson, eds., *Change in the International System*, Chapter 1. Boulder, Colo.: Westview Press.

Index